KT-437-618

# New

# FOWLER
# PROFICIENCY

# READING

## W. S. FOWLER

NEW EDITIONS

A40572

First published by New Editions 2002

New Editions                New Editions
37 Bagley Wood Road         PO Box 76101
Kennington                  17110 Nea Smyrni
Oxford OX1 5LY              Athens
England                     Greece

Tel: (+3 010) 9883156
Fax: (+3 010) 9880223
E-mail: enquiries@new-editions.com
Internet: www.new-editions.com

© W. S. Fowler 2002

ISBN 960-403-032-9      Student's Book
ISBN 960-403-031-0      Teacher's Book

A 40572
EALING TERTIARY COLLEGE
ACTON CENTRE LIBRARY

All rights reserved. No part of this publication may be reproduced, stored in a retrieval system, or transmitted in any form or by any means, electronic, mechanical, photocopying, recording, or otherwise, without the prior written permission of the publishers. Any person who carries out any unauthorised act in relation to this publication may be liable to criminal prosecution and civil claims for damages.

**Acknowledgements**

We are grateful to the following for permission to reproduce copyright material:

Nicholas Coleridge for his article 'Wish I was always here' published in The Telegraph on 13 August 2001.

Financial Times Ltd for extracts from the articles '19m poppadoms a day and rising' by Beatrice Newbery, 21.07.01, 'In deep water' by Clive Cookson, 28.07.01.

Independent Newspapers (UK) Ltd for extracts from the articles 'Shrine of America's Leaders' by Mary Dejevsky, 07.07.01, 'New boules, please' by John Litchfield, 14.07.01.

Telegraph Group Ltd for extracts from the articles 'If you want to keep moving, ban buses' by Minette Marrin, 14.07.01, 'Life's a beach hut' by Josie Barnard, 21.07.01, 'Where the wildlife is' by Julie Davidson, 23.09.01, 'Love at first sight' by Caroline McGhee, 22.07.01, book review: 'Circle of sisters' by Kathryn Hughes, 'Born to be together' by Jane Bond, 25.05.01, 'Testing the water – do spas work?' by Cassandra Jardine, 09.07.01, 'Indiana Jones - and the lost scout' by Judith Woods, 13.07.01, 'Boredom is the best lesson of all' by Victoria Hislop, 21.07.01, 'And off she went to the circus' by Amanda Mitchison, 08.07.01, 'Armchair sportsfan' 08.07.01, 'A jolly good sort' by David Jenkins, 05.08.01, 'Motorcycle menace' by Andrew Morgan, © Telegraph Group Limited 2001.

New International Newspapers Ltd for extracts from the articles 'Hounded into office' by Vanora Bennet, © The Times, 19.05.01, 'Not so elementary, my dear Watson' by Marcel Berlins, © The Times, 'What Mozart had and Tracy hasn't' by Roger Scruton, © The Sunday Times, 20.05.01, 'Suspect held over murder of Fossey' by Jon Swain, © The Sunday Times, 29.07.01, 'Show on the road' by Hugh Pearman, © The Sunday Times, 20.08.01, 'A sexy young woman who danced until dawn' by Sally Kinnes, © The Sunday Times, 19.08.01.

Every effort has been made to trace copyright holders. If any have been inadvertently overlooked, the publishers will be pleased to make the necessary acknowledgements at the first opportunity.

## INTRODUCTION

### General

The format of the reading paper in the revised Proficiency examination shows a number of changes, and is now as follows:

| Part 1 | Three texts, each containing six multiple-choice vocabulary questions | (one mark each, 18 in all) |
|--------|----------------------------------------------------------------------|----------------------------|
| Part 2 | Four short texts, each containing two multiple-choice comprehension questions | (two marks each, 16 in all) |
| Part 3 | Gapped text, with seven paragraphs to be put back in the correct place | (two marks each, 14 in all) |
| Part 4 | One long text containing seven multiple-choice comprehension questions | (two marks each, 14 in all) |

The total mark possible is 62, the time allowed is one hour 30 minutes, and a reasonable score equivalent to a pass on this paper would be 40-45.

There are two main differences from the previous format. The vocabulary questions, instead of being tested in separate sentences, now appear in three short passages. This provides greater contextualisation, and also has the effect of shifting the emphasis away from words misunderstood because of first-language interference towards expressions that frequently occur in modern English, such as phrasal verbs and common combinations of verb, noun and adjective. The second main difference is that comprehension is now not only tested by means of multiple-choice questions and a greater variety of texts are employed.

In both cases, success in this part of the examination depends on wide reading and on adopting the correct techniques to deal with the different kinds of question. The right answers to the vocabulary questions do not depend on translation or on having learnt a very large number of words in English but on recognising that you have seen a word or phrase used in a particular context or in combination with others. In terms of reading comprehension, it is essential to follow right approach, as indicated below.

### Organisation

This book contains 20 units relating in form and content to the Reading paper of the examination. Four of the units are practice tests, which have been thoroughly pretested with students preparing for the examination, and follow the examination format exactly. The other 16 units contain:

Part 1: Three texts with multiple choice vocabulary questions and a Vocabulary Development exercise which demonstrates why incorrect answers are incorrect and in what context they would be correct.

Part 2: two, rather than four, short texts with two multiple-choice comprehension questions each

either  Part 3: gapped text (ordering paragraphs)

or  Part 4: longer text with multiple-choice comprehension questions

Part 3 and Part 4 appear in alternate units.

In addition to the 20 basic units, there are 20 exercises revising vocabulary items that have previously appeared, and three appendixes listing and defining all the phrasal verbs, common combinations of words and idiomatic expressions that appear in the book.

### Content

The themes of the passages reflect those indicated by the examiners as of most importance and are identical with those chosen for the companion volume, *New Fowler Proficiency Listening and Speaking*. If the books are used in conjunction with each other, the essential vocabulary required can be consistently recycled and put into practice in students' production of language in speech and writing.

The longer passages have been selected from the kind of journalism found in quality newspapers, which forms the basis for most examination items, and the others are based on topics of general interest relating to the themes. In all there are 148 texts covering a wide variety of subjects and language, contextualising the material.

### Advice

Tips are provided in the book when different types of question appear for the first time to aid students in the correct techniques. The main points are summarised here:

### Part 1

Almost every correct answer depends on recognition. You have seen the word before used in a certain context or in combination with others. Particular attention needs to be paid to prepositions accompanying verbs or in collocations, combined with nouns, since this may determine whether an answer is correct or not. Students should learn the phrases in the appendixes as phrases, not as separate words, and should keep a note book listing any similar phrases they encounter in their reading.

### Parts 2 and 4

The key to success is to take enough time to read the passages carefully before looking at the questions. Then decide which part of the text each question refers to and check the choices against it, one by one. Most questions either rephrase what is said in the text or ask what is being said in a paragraph in general terms.

### Part 3

This form of question is new to the Proficiency examination. Read the text on the left to get a general idea of what the passage is about, and try to decide what sort of information is missing. Do not read the missing paragraphs one by one, but try to find one that fills each gap in turn. The content may provide the answer, but there are other clues, which are grammatical. If a paragraph begins *He* or *This*, what is missing must refer either to an appropriate man or action.

# Contents

3W    428.4 FOW    A40572

# Contents

# Contents

# Contents

**Tip**

*When choosing the answer for questions 1–3, think: Have I seen any of the words in a combination with others before? If so, it's probably the right answer.*

## Part 1

For questions 1–18, read the texts and decide which answer (**A**, **B**, **C** or **D**) best fits each gap.

### BLOOD IS THICKER THAN PRINCIPLES

The present government is committed to promoting state education at the (1) .............. of private schools but not, it seems, when ministers' own children are concerned. The Prime Minister (2) .............. the pattern by sending his eldest son to an independent school and many of his supporters have followed (3) .............. . The Prime Minister used the excuse of religion, but if Tristan and Lavinia prove too (4) .............. for the rough-and-tumble of the state-school playground, that is sufficient cause for them to be removed, (5) .............. much it costs. As some party members privately admit, in a choice between your children and your principles, the children must (6) .............. first.

| | | | | | | | |
|---|---|---|---|---|---|---|---|
| 1 | **A** cost | **B** expense | **C** loss | **D** price |
| 2 | **A** drew | **B** made | **C** put | **D** set |
| 3 | **A** example | **B** lead | **C** suit | **D** mould |
| 4 | **A** sensible | **B** sensitive | **C** sentimental | **D** sensational |
| 5 | **A** however | **B** for how | **C** whatever | **D** no matter |
| 6 | **A** come | **B** go | **C** place | **D** take |

### WHY CAN'T OUR CHILDREN READ?

The new national reading programme for beginners, aimed at reversing the decline in literacy, emphasises rules and the sounds of individual words. Traditionalists will no doubt heave a (7) .............. of relief at what they will regard as a return to the good old (8) .............. . Their opponents argue, however, that the texts used for this purpose years ago (9) .............. no relationship to real life and (10) .............. short of the basic requirement for any learning materials: they should (11) .............. interest in what is being taught. Educators must not lose (12) .............. of the fact that teaching rules without taking this into account will not solve the problem.

| | | | | | | | |
|---|---|---|---|---|---|---|---|
| 7 | **A** groan | **B** sob | **C** sigh | **D** breath |
| 8 | **A** period | **B** days | **C** times | **D** years |
| 9 | **A** bore | **B** carried | **C** held | **D** kept |
| 10 | **A** dropped | **B** fell | **C** ran | **D** failed |
| 11 | **A** arise | **B** arouse | **C** raise | **D** rise |
| 12 | **A** grasp | **B** regard | **C** vision | **D** sight |

## TEACHERS' PRESENTS

When I was at school in England years ago, it would never have (13) ............... my parents' minds to buy presents for the teachers. It was not until I started to teach abroad that I was a little taken (14) ............... the first Christmas to find the class had clubbed together to buy me something.

In Britain, however, following in the (15) ............... of American parents, it has evidently become the done thing to give teachers presents and in affluent private schools the custom has got so much out of (16) ............... that mothers rival one another in choosing expensive gifts. Parents who are not so well off naturally take a (17) ............... view of this since, in these days of (18) ............... assessment of pupils replacing final exams, it comes perilously close to bribery.

| | | | | | | | |
|---|---|---|---|---|---|---|---|
| 13 | A | crossed | B | entered | C | passed | D | informed |
| 14 | A | apart | B | behind | C | aback | D | surprised |
| 15 | A | lead | B | leaf | C | footsteps | D | footprints |
| 16 | A | scale | B | form | C | range | D | hand |
| 17 | A | dark | B | dim | C | black | D | bad |
| 18 | A | continuous | B | immediate | C | consecutive | D | repetitive |

**Tip**

*Did you get any of questions 4–6 wrong? If so, compare the first three sentences in Vocabulary Development. Make a note of the differences.*

## Vocabulary Development

Complete the sentences below with a word or phrase taken from the choices for the questions you have answered. The sentences are printed in the same order as the questions. Note the difference between the correct answer below and a phrase of similar meaning in the passages above.

1   The tabloid press is fond of using ................................... headlines.

2   I'm prepared to pay the price, ................................... it costs.

3   In a decision of this kind, your children must ................................... first place.

4   The audience greeted the announcement that the star of the play was unable to appear with a ............................ of disappointment.

5   What a pleasure to see you at the reunion! It's just like old ................................... .

6   Difficulties in reading often ................................... because the children are not interested in the subject.

7   It would never have ................................... my mother's head to buy a present for my teacher.

8   British parents seem to have taken a ................................... out of the Americans' book.

9   He threw a stone at the rat but it was already out of ................................... .

10   The exams will take place on three ................................... days, from Monday to Wednesday.

## Part 2

These two texts are concerned with an aspect of education. For questions **19–22**, choose the answer (**A**, **B**, **C** or **D**) which you think fits best according to the text.

### THE PLUS AND MINUS OF FURTHER EDUCATION COLLEGES

The traditional view of further education colleges is that they represent the last chance for those who can't make it at school. Drop-outs have to have somewhere to drop, and these colleges, with their slack rules, are the ideal location for teenagers who just want to hang around for a couple of years with nothing to do.

Yet precisely because these colleges are less rigorous in the demands they make of students, they offer advantages to some young people, especially those who rebel against discipline, are interested in less conventional subjects and think themselves sufficiently grown-up to resent having to call another adult 'Mr' or 'Miss'.

If measured by examination results leading to university entrance, schools do far better but this is in part due to the fact that colleges accept all-comers. Advice to parents should be based on the needs of their children. Those who get on well with the standard subjects in the curriculum are better off at school; those who are aiming eventually at vocational training will probably be more at home in an FE college.

**19**    What does the writer say is the traditional view of further education colleges?

    **A**    They were set up to help teenagers with problems.

    **B**    They are a complete waste of time.

    **C**    They are the final opportunity for those who have failed at school.

    **D**    Their lack of discipline encourages students to be lazy.

**20**    What sort of student is likely to benefit most from going to an FE college?

    **A**    one who is very mature for his/her age

    **B**    one who is interested in a less conventional career

    **C**    one who cannot stand being told what to do

    **D**    one who just wants to enjoy life

### Tip

*Always read the text carefully before looking at the questions. Then look at the question to see which part of the text it refers to.*

*For question 19, which of the choices says the same thing as the first sentence of the passage?*

## SCHOOLS FOR PARENTS

When the government started promoting parenting classes a few years ago, most parents regarded it as typical of the nanny state, poking its nose into things that were none of its business. It was almost as if they had been invented as a means of punishing parents for their children's misbehaviour. But now they are all the rage. There has been an explosion of interest in courses aimed at teaching parents how to deal with unmanageable adolescents.

As in most conflictive situations, parents begin by listening sympathetically but when they are driven frantic by rudeness or simply being ignored, scream and shout until they fall silent, horrified that they themselves are 'behaving like kids'. The answer is to explain what is needed for co-operation sensibly and calmly, and afterwards to be firm and consistent. But it isn't likely, after fifteen years of spoiling the child, that the situation will change overnight.

### Active Vocabulary List

These are some words and phrases commonly connected with the subject of education. If you are not sure of the meaning of any words or phrases, look them up in your dictionary.

> *nursery school / kindergarten*
> *primary school*
> *secondary school / high school*
> *university (college, USA)*
> *adult education*
> *state / private education*
> *pupil / student*
> *class / form / year*
> *class / lesson*
> *term (semester, USA)*
> *lecture, seminar*
> *qualification, degree*
> *doctorate*
> *educational, academic*

**21**   The initial reaction to parenting classes was that the Government

   **A**   was trying to protect parents from their children.

   **B**   was trying to help parents understand them.

   **C**   was interfering in family life.

   **D**   was taking the easy way out by blaming parents.

**22**   The best chance for parents to improve their relationship with adolescents is to

   **A**   lay down reasonable rules for behaviour and stick to them.

   **B**   recognise the defects in their own behaviour and apologise.

   **C**   keep quiet, rather than have an argument.

   **D**   try to put themselves in their children's situation.

**Tip**

*The same rule applies to long texts as to short ones. Always read the text carefully before looking at the questions.*

## Part 3 (Multiple-choice comprehension)

Read this article about children in the school holidays. For questions **23–29**, choose the answer (**A, B, C or D**) which you think fits best according to the text.

### BOREDOM IS THE BEST LESSON OF ALL

The first day of the school holidays is a defining moment in the year. Unlike the first day of spring, a vague date that nobody can quite agree on, the beginning of the long vacation is a precise point in the children's calendar. The next six or seven weeks stretch out beyond the reach of the imagination and, as far as they're concerned, the end of the holiday is light years off – so distant that, by the time they return to school, they'll probably have grown at least a couple of shoe sizes.

Now that I am a parent, I can still share that 'Day one of the holidays' sense of anticipation and enjoy the respite from the rigid daily routine of drop-offs, pick-ups and homework deadlines just as much as the children. But the pure pleasure of it all can be as short-lived as an ice cream in a heat wave. Within hours, you'll detect the first signs of boredom (not usually very subtle, since they're accompanied by that plaintive wail, 'Muuum, I'm bored'). Suddenly, the prospect of the forthcoming weeks takes on a whole new complexion. If you were setting off on the London marathon having jogged once round the park, you'd be better prepared.

So how should we react? If our response is anything like our own parents', we'll tell them to run along and occupy themselves. For us, this meant many hours of kicking our heels, an activity that was an acceptable part of childhood and, in retrospect, a very enjoyable one. Unquestionably, we could be left more to our own devices 20 or 30 years ago. It's not simply nostalgic nonsense to say that it was perfectly safe for us as 10-year-olds to go off in a gang for the day on our bikes with a sandwich and a soft drink. This is what we did, most days.

Whatever other changes have or haven't taken place, there are many more cars today than there were in the 1970s and they now drive at speeds that make cycling for children a dangerous sport. Few of us would send a child under 10 off to the playground with the casual

words: 'Have fun and make sure you're back before dark.' It's as archaic as Little Red Riding Hood going off into the woods all on her own to visit Grandma.

There are, then, some good reasons why we feel duty-bound to provide our children with entertainment and why there is a sense of parental responsibility to alleviate their boredom. But many of us would also harbour some kind of fear that our offspring will suffer irreparable damage if they aren't engaged in organised activity.

For the ambitious parent (or the working parent or the parents who just feel that the child will benefit from being out of their hair) the long vacation can be one non-stop, helter-skelter series of courses and residential weeks at summer camps, the whole period conducted with the same rhythm as the school term. Here is another learning opportunity, we're tempted to think, a chance to make sure they stay up with the leaders. If we aren't careful, the long holiday can turn into a two-month opportunity for parents to drive their children around the country and themselves into the ground.

Even if we haven't created a schedule of events for the children, what is it about boredom that we fear for our children? Perhaps we need to calm down and resist the panic which seizes us whenever the 'B' word rears its ugly head. Boredom is the space where planned activity stops and something spontaneous begins, and where the children start to draw on their own resources.

Boredom will drive children to make up their own games, with their own rules and logic, and, if there aren't enough players, they will introduce some imaginary ones. Siblings might even begin to display uncharacteristic interest in each other, needing reinforcements for a game or extras for a play. When we were children and there seemed to be nothing to do, we would loaf about until we thought of something and, if we hadn't a friend around for the day, we would make up an imaginary one. I had one who hung around for years.

As everyone's French teacher told them, 'to be bored' (*s'ennuyer*) is a reflexive verb. If you were bored, you had only yourself to blame. Boredom is a fact of life and the sooner children realise that there isn't a magic pill to dispel it, the better. As the novelist A N Wilson put it: 'Boredom is what most human lives consist of. Few jobs are interesting all of the time, and when retirement age has been reached, the long days of emptiness cannot possibly be entirely devoid of tedium. Learning how to cope with these periods of vacancy can actually reduce or eliminate their boringness.'

Clearly, you can't absolve yourself of all responsibility for keeping the children occupied. But you should allow plenty of room for boredom. It could be as much of an education as ... their education.

*Article by Victoria Hislop, © Telegraph Group Limited*

**23** What does the writer say about children's reaction to the beginning of the long summer holidays?

   **A** They know they will start on a certain date.

   **B** They cannot imagine when they will end.

   **C** They know they will grow a lot during this time.

   **D** They find it difficult to recognise the changes in the seasons.

**24** How do the reactions of parents like the writer change after the first impression?

   **A** They have the same sense of excitement as the children.

   **B** They are delighted that they no longer have to take them to school.

   **C** They realise that they have made no preparations for amusing them.

   **D** They realise that they are in poor physical condition for entertaining them.

**25** What does the writer suggest that her own mother said to her if she complained of being bored?

   **A** 'Find something to do.'

   **B** 'Get out from under my feet.'

   **C** 'Why don't you join a gang?'

   **D** 'Go for a ride.'

**26** Why does she think that parents nowadays are unwilling to adopt the same attitudes?

   **A** They are afraid of children being alone.

   **B** They are afraid of them being out after dark.

   **C** They know that the roads are no longer safe.

   **D** They know that playgrounds are no longer safe.

**27** Why are some parents keen on children taking part in a series of organised activities throughout the summer?

   **A** They are afraid that the children will be injured if left to themselves.

   **B** They want them out of the house in order to enjoy their own interests.

   **C** They think it is essential for them to continue their studies on holiday.

   **D** They are afraid that in some way they will fall behind their classmates.

**28** What, in the writer's opinion, is the main advantage of children being bored?

   **A** They are compelled to develop their own imagination.

   **B** They realise that they need their brothers and sisters.

   **C** They make friends more easily.

   **D** They devote more time to useful experiments.

**29** In what way is it suggested that boredom is a necessary preparation for adult life?

   **A** If you are bored, it is your own fault.

   **B** Life itself is boring.

   **C** There are bound to be periods of inactivity in any existence.

   **D** When you get old, you will not have very much to do.

> **Tip**
>
> *The form of question 25 is perhaps new to you. Find the reference to the writer's parents' response. Which phrase comes closest to the meaning of 'run along and occupy themselves'?*

## Part I

For questions 1–18, read the texts and decide which answer (**A**, **B**, **C** or **D**) best fits each gap.

### THE WORLD'S MOST FAMOUS SMILE

The Mona Lisa is probably the world's (1) ...............-known picture, but it is at first (2) ............... extraordinary that this rather plump Florentine housewife should have obtained such celebrity. She looks ordinary even beside other females that Leonardo da Vinci himself painted, (3) ............... the model for Botticelli's *Venus*.

The Romantic writers of nineteenth-century Paris were mainly responsible. They were obsessed with the idea of the *femme fatale*, the woman who tempts men and leads them (4) ............... and identified the type with Mona Lisa's (5) ............... smile. Once the myth was established, publicity did the (6) ............... .

| 1 | **A** better | **B** best | **C** more | **D** most |
|---|---|---|---|---|
| 2 | **A** impression | **B** look | **C** sight | **D** view |
| 3 | **A** let alone | **B** leave alone | **C** let apart | **D** leave apart |
| 4 | **A** wrong | **B** wide | **C** mad | **D** astray |
| 5 | **A** enigmatic | **B** puzzled | **C** obscure | **D** unclear |
| 6 | **A** effect | **B** result | **C** rest | **D** remainder |

### THE GENIUS WHO PAINTED EVERYDAY LIFE

If Leonardo is the artist whose name has come to stand (7) ............... universal genius, Vermeer is perhaps the greatest unknown. We know (8) ............... nothing about this man, born in Delft in Holland in 1632.

It was not until the late 19th century that his genius was recognised. The painstaking work of identifying which of the pictures (9) ............... to him were (10) ............... began. One reason for their being worth millions today is that they proved to be (11) ............... and far between. While his contemporaries produced 50 canvases in a year, Vermeer only managed two or three. But they are among the most satisfying works of art ever painted, (12) ............... to us above all because of their calm reassurance of the solid virtues of everyday life.

| 7 | **A** for | **B** in for | **C** up for | **D** out for |
|---|---|---|---|---|
| 8 | **A** nearly | **B** next to | **C** hardly | **D** only |
| 9 | **A** accounted | **B** claimed | **C** referred | **D** attributed |
| 10 | **A** official | **B** veritable | **C** genuine | **D** faithful |
| 11 | **A** few | **B** little | **C** seldom | **D** uncommon |
| 12 | **A** attracting | **B** appealing | **C** alluring | **D** charming |

### Tip

*The answer to question 7 is a phrasal verb. Learn the phrasal verbs in Appendix 1. Compare your answer to question 4 in the Vocabulary Development exercise.*

## THE DAY OF THE TRIFFIDS

John Wyndham (1903-69) was among the first science fiction writers but his work has never been (13) .............. .
In *The Day of the Triffids* (1951), he imagined Great Britain overrun by (14) ............... plants able to walk and to
(15) ............... with each other. The human population is helpless because almost everyone has been blinded by
a flash in the sky.

The novel was written in the (16) ............... of the first atomic bomb but is equally (17) ............... to our situation
today. The plants and the flash are both the result of experiments that go wrong. The novel strikes a warning
(18) ............... for scientists and politicians who experiment with things they do not fully understand.

| 13 | **A** exceeded | **B** improved | **C** outclassed | **D** surpassed |
|---|---|---|---|---|
| 14 | **A** deadly | **B** mortal | **C** killing | **D** fatal |
| 15 | **A** contact | **B** communicate | **C** transmit | **D** correspond |
| 16 | **A** consequence | **B** sequel | **C** aftermath | **D** epilogue |
| 17 | **A** critical | **B** serious | **C** urgent | **D** relevant |
| 18 | **A** sound | **B** tone | **C** note | **D** beat |

## Vocabulary Development

Complete the sentences below with a word or phrase taken from the choices for the questions you have answered.
The sentences are printed in the same order as the questions. Note the difference between the correct answer
below and a phrase of similar meaning in the passages above.

1   My first ..................................... of the Mona Lisa was that she wasn't very attractive.

2   She was the sort of woman that drives men ..................................... .

3   She looked at me with a ..................................... expression, evidently failing to understand what I meant.

4   Mr Jones is ill so I'd like you to stand ..................................... him and take his class.

5   We know ..................................... anything about Vermeer.

6   Once he became famous, many collectors ..................................... that paintings in their possession were by Vermeer.

7   In my opinion, no one has ever ..................................... on Wyndham's science fiction novels.

8   Several people died in a ..................................... road accident yesterday.

9   If I haven't got your address or telephone number, how am I going to ..................................... you?

10  Not long ago another novelist published a ..................................... to *The Day of the Triffids*, beginning where that
    novel ends.

## Part 2

These two texts are concerned with different aspects of the arts. For questions **19–22**, choose the answer (**A, B, C** or **D**) which you think fits best according to the text.

### RESTORE OR RUIN

Restorers of paintings aim to clean works of art to reveal the artist's original intentions. But far too often, they alter them irretrievably. The latest controversy of this kind concerns five Titians lent to the National Gallery of Scotland. Critics say that, as a result of successive attempts to clean them, they are pale imitations of the original.

Perhaps the most infamous case of the past was that of the Elgin Marbles, which were scrubbed in the 1930s to make them look whiter, removing their original texture. When Michelangelo's ceiling in the Sistine Chapel was restored, the glazes used to soften the colours came away with the dirt, making them too bright. And layer after layer has been stripped from Leonardo Da Vinci's painting of the Last Supper, though this was already endangered in his lifetime because of his risky technique.

---

**19**   What is the main criticism of the restoration of the paintings by Titian?

   **A**   They have been cleaned too frequently.

   **B**   The Gallery had no right to clean paintings that did not belong to it.

   **C**   The paintings look like copies.

   **D**   The original colours and tones have faded.

**20**   Which of these artists was partly responsible for the poor state of his work?

   **A**   Titian

   **B**   Michelangelo

   **C**   Leonardo Da Vinci

   **D**   The artist of the Elgin Marbles

### FRIENDS OR FOES

The great American novelists, Scott Fitzgerald and Ernest Hemingway, were friendly for a time but their attraction was one of opposites. Fitzgerald was already famous when he introduced Hemingway to his publisher with a flood of compliments, bowled over by the younger man's powerful personality. His reward in later years, as his own star waned and Hemingway's rose, was for Hemingway to dismiss him as 'a butterfly'.

The relationship between the two men expressed the contrast between them. The more sensitive Fitzgerald wasted his talent, drifting into alcoholism and self-pity, while Hemingway was brutally competitive in everything he did. One needed to be humiliated, the other to humiliate.

**21**  Why is the relationship between the two writers described as the attraction of opposites?

    **A**    Because Fitzgerald was already well known when they met.

    **B**    Because Fitzgerald admired Hemingway.

    **C**    Because their careers moved in opposite directions.

    **D**    Because their personalities were very different.

**22**  What attitude was Hemingway expressing in calling Fitzgerald a butterfly?

    **A**    ingratitude

    **B**    contempt

    **C**    envy

    **D**    rivalry

> **Tip**
>
> *Some questions depend on a knowledge of vocabulary that does not appear in the text. If you are not sure of the meaning of any of the choices here, look them up in your dictionary.*

---

**Active Vocabulary List**

These are some words and phrases commonly connected with the subject of the arts. If you are not sure of the meaning of any words or phrases, look them up in your dictionary.

**art**
still life, landscape
classical, impressionist
artist, painter, sculptor

painting, drawing, watercolour
masterpiece, abstract, modern
sculpture, statue
museum, art gallery, exhibition

**music**
classical, jazz, pop, rock, folk
conductor, musician, singer
composer, songwriter, lyrics

orchestra, choir, band
concert, performance
opera, libretto

**literature**
novel, biography, short story, poem
author, novelist, biographer, poet
character, hero, heroine

science fiction, detective story, thriller
narrative, dialogue, style

### Part 3 (Ordering paragraphs)

This article consists of 15 paragraphs. Seven of them have been removed. Choose from the paragraphs **A-H** the one that fits each gap (**23-29**). There is one extra paragraph that does not fit and which you do not need to use.

## WHAT MOZART HAD AND TRACY HASN'T

A liturgy of opposites has developed in the theory of education; creativity versus routine, spontaneity versus rote learning, innovation versus conformity. In the face of all the evidence to the contrary, educationalists go on telling us that children learn not by conforming to some external standard, but by 'releasing their inner potential' and expressing their creative skills. Hence, rote learning, facts and traditional routines are dismissed as irrelevant.

**23**

Imagine an educational guru who told us that nothing mattered in mathematics so much as creativity. The great mathematicians of the past were distinguished, the guru tells us, by their imaginative powers. They were able to break through the hide-bound rules of their predecessors, to cast aside the ordinary routines of proof, and to take an imaginative leap to their conclusions. We should therefore be teaching our children to release their mathematical creativity and to value spontaneity against rule-following. We all know what such a philosophy would entail in practice – namely, ignorance.

**24**

Why do we think that things are so different in the case of language, literature, history and the arts? The answer is to be found in the long tradition of woolly thinking that began with Rousseau. On the one hand, educationists believe, there is the objective world of facts, and this we must explore through disciplined learning and the building of theories. On the other hand, there is the subjective world of opinions, feelings and artistic urges, to be explored through self-expression,

**25**

Such thinking is contradicted by the obvious fact that self-expression is not innate but acquired: the self, too, is a social product. We do children a great wrong by withholding the discipline, the knowledge and the store of examples that confer the art of self-expression, since, by doing so, we damage the self. The anger of many young people leaving school is the anger of the inarticulate. The emphasis on the creative act produces teenagers specialising in acts of destruction.

**26**

Of course Mozarts are few and far between, but it is all the more reason to be as disciplined as Mozart. With the discipline, there is the chance of being creative; without it, there is no chance at all. Visit a British art school today and you are almost certain to find an array of objects, maybe just an old coat with the artist's name tag pinned to it – all praised and rewarded for their 'creativity' and all as dull and empty as the work of caged chimpanzees.

**27**

Of course, artistic ability is not like scientific knowledge: you cannot acquire it merely by diligent study. There comes a point where a leap of the imagination is required. If in music, art or poetry you say something that has already been said, then you say nothing. In Ezra Pound's famous dictum, you have to 'make it new', and that means imprinting your words, your notes or your forms with a distinct personality and an inimitable life. But what is so striking about the art works produced on a diet of unadulterated creativity is not that they are new and surprising, but drawn from a repertoire of clichés already done to death by modernists, and now reduced to a routine.

**28**

Real originality does not defy convention but depends on it. You can only 'make it new' when the newness is perceivable, which means departing from conventions while at the same time affirming them. Hence originality requires tradition if it is to make artistic sense.

**29**

People who have learnt poetry by rote and know how to compose the occasional sonnet may not revolutionise the consciousness of mankind as Shakespeare did. But they are more likely to understand what great writers are saying, are likely to live on a more exalted plane as a result of doing so, and are also able, through their life and example, to make a positive contribution in the great war against Dullness.

*Article by Roger Scruton, © The Sunday Times*

**A** Hardly an art school in our country now insists on figurative drawing, clay modelling, casting, or the mastery of pigments – still less a knowledge of art history, or an ability to discern just why the planes of a Matisse interior intersect at an acute angle, or the shadows of a Constable are done in yellows and browns.

**B** Any other approach is considered 'authoritarian'. Grammar, style, art, even history, are all alleged to be matters of opinion. Hence the purpose of education is to give children the confidence to express their subjective attitudes to these things – subjective attitudes being all that we have.

**C** Children write poetry before they have memorised a single line of it, dance before they have learnt a single step, paint and daub without the faintest knowledge of figurative drawing. Grammar, spelling and punctuation are degraded in the interests of creative self-expression.

**D** But what about the rest of us? Why should we, who are not geniuses, acquire the knowledge needed by those who are? This is a difficult question, but I like to believe that people who acquire artistic, musical or literary skills, but who lack the divine spark, are nevertheless an addition to the common good.

**E** The shibboleth of creativity has been especially counter-productive in the arts. Consider Mozart, whose ever-fresh, ever-lucid melodies are among the most original creations of mankind. Mozart did not become a creative genius merely by letting it all hang out, even though he had more to hang out than anyone. He was rigorously and relentlessly schooled by his father, subjected to the ordeal of public performances, trained in the art of memory and the grammar of the classical style.

**F** But will we never learn that what really separates the great artists of the past from those who claim to be 'creative' today is rigorous education? The exhibits of such 'creative artists' as Damien Hurst and Tracey Emin lack the skills required for real art and are shockingly banal. Shocking is apparently both the be-all and end-all of the intention but in the long run the result is not so much shocking as dull.

**G** You can be a creative genius in mathematics only if you have acquired the discipline of mathematical proof. In teaching science, even educationists seem prepared to admit that discipline comes first, creativity last. They recognise that chemistry taught with a regime of pure self-expression would soon degenerate into alchemy, just as 'creative physics' would be hard to distinguish from witchcraft.

**H** The myth that we are all instinctively creative goes hand in hand with the belief in originality as the sole criterion of artistic merit. And, when rules and disciplines are rejected, the only proof of originality becomes the ability to shock or surprise. Nothing that Mozart did was intended to shock his audience, or to surprise them with some outrageous gesture. The originality of his music is inseparable from its rule-guided objectivity.

**Tip**

*For those who have not done this kind of exercise before, here is some guidance on how to begin:*

*1) Read the text on the left to understand the general line of argument. What is the writer saying about the difference between great artists and British artists today?*

*2) Paragraphs 1 and 2 are about teaching children. Does any paragraph on the right refer to teaching children?*

*3) Paragraph 3 begins by suggesting the arts are like other subjects. What are they? Is there a paragraph on the right that mentions them?*

*4) Paragraphs 4 and 5 begin with two very common kinds of clue. Paragraph 4 begins 'Such thinking...'. What is missing must refer to an attitude to education. Paragraph 5 mentions someone by name – Mozart. The missing paragraph must introduce his name.*

## Part I

For questions **1–18**, read the texts and decide which answer (**A**, **B**, **C** or **D**) best fits each gap.

### THE INTERPRETER

There are in effect three careers open to those with a (1) .............. for languages: teacher, translator or interpreter, and interpreter is the one that appeals to those who (2) .............. the limelight. But it is by no means all (3) .............. sailing. Most speakers seem unaware of the fact that someone is trying to (4) .............. what they are saying into another language at speed. The worst of them mumble so that it is almost impossible to (5) .............. out what they are saying, but the greatest problem you have is when you realise that what they are saying is nonsense, but you know that you must not give (6) .............. to the temptation to leap out of the booth and shout: 'That's rubbish, and you know it.'

| | | | | | | | | |
|---|---|---|---|---|---|---|---|---|
| 1 | **A** | fitness | **B** | flair | **C** | skill | **D** | tendency |
| 2 | **A** | crave | **B** | beg | **C** | wish | **D** | plead |
| 3 | **A** | clear | **B** | straight | **C** | easy | **D** | plain |
| 4 | **A** | adapt | **B** | alter | **C** | convert | **D** | resume |
| 5 | **A** | give | **B** | make | **C** | point | **D** | take |
| 6 | **A** | over | **B** | up | **C** | place | **D** | way |

### IS YOUR RESEARCH REALLY NECESSARY?

According to ex-President Clinton, the (7) .............. of human knowledge now doubles every five years. This estimate was apparently based on the number of scientific articles published, but how many of these really contain anything useful? It may (8) .............. to the specialist in the field that we now know the exact dimensions of dinosaurs that became (9) .............. millions of years ago but the rest of us just (10) .............. in the information, shrug, and change the (11) .............. . The justification given for all this obscure activity is that something valuable may emerge from it. That is all very well as far as it (12) .............. but if Clinton's calculation had referred only to useful human knowledge, it would not have seemed so impressive.

| | | | | | | | | |
|---|---|---|---|---|---|---|---|---|
| 7 | **A** | quantity | **B** | heap | **C** | store | **D** | bulk |
| 8 | **A** | count | **B** | interest | **C** | matter | **D** | value |
| 9 | **A** | extinct | **B** | perished | **C** | buried | **D** | deceased |
| 10 | **A** | let | **B** | take | **C** | put | **D** | allow |
| 11 | **A** | subject | **B** | theme | **C** | topic | **D** | text |
| 12 | **A** | runs | **B** | carries | **C** | goes | **D** | holds |

## How to succeed with the BBC

At one time a BBC presenter's (13) ............... description was clear. Apart from being intelligent and well-informed, you were expected to be good-looking and to have a universally (14) ............... accent. But a survey suggesting that the BBC is believed to be elitist and out of (15) ............... led to its issuing a book that contradicts previous assumptions. Surprisingly, reporters are encouraged to break the (16) ............... . The custom of monopolising the centre of the screen, suggesting that they are more important than the story they have to tell, is (17) ............... . The idea is that the BBC should look and sound more approachable. But the question remains as to whether this is just (18) ............... dressing or whether they really mean it.

| 13 | **A** work | **B** job | **C** task | **D** skill |
|----|-----------|-----------|-----------|-----------|
| 14 | **A** apprehensible | **B** comprehensible | **C** recognisable | **D** distinguishable |
| 15 | **A** reach | **B** order | **C** range | **D** touch |
| 16 | **A** rules | **B** codes | **C** standards | **D** laws |
| 17 | **A** disused | **B** dispensed | **C** discarded | **D** discharged |
| 18 | **A** fancy | **B** stage | **C** shop | **D** window |

## Vocabulary Development

Complete the sentences below with a word or phrase taken from the choices for the questions you have answered. The sentences are printed in the same order as the questions. Note the difference between the correct answer below and a phrase of similar meaning in the passages above.

1  Good speakers ................................... their message to the kind of audience they are facing.

2  I had to ................................... out to the interpreter the mistake in her translation.

3  Even when you find the task very difficult, you must not give ................................... .

4  When he joined the research team, the ................................... of the work had already been done.

5  That sort of project may ................................... the specialist, but no one else.

6  Some of the details of his thesis are doubtful but his main argument ................................... .

7  He had changed so much that his face was hardly ................................... .

8  You should keep those medicines out of the children's ................................... .

9  Everyone in the hall could hear him so he ................................... with the microphone.

10  We're all wearing ................................... dress at the party, so I'm going as a Roman.

## Part 2

These two texts are concerned with different professions. For questions **19–22**, choose the answer (**A**, **B**, **C** or **D**) which you think fits best according to the text.

### A CAREER IN ASTRONOMY

The 1960s were an excellent time to start a career in astronomy because new discoveries were being made all the time. Very distant parts of the universe were coming into view for the first time, and the first strong clues had been received that the entire cosmos began with a big bang. Nowadays, nearly everyone in the field subscribes to this theory that the universe started off in a hot, dense state at a given moment in the past, but the pace of discovery has not slowed down at all. In recent years, there has been a great improvement in the

sharpness and clarity of pictures received. Telescopes today reveal galaxies so far away that their light takes millions of years to reach us. There could not be a better time for a young cosmologist, and there is still work for the veterans to do.

When we look at the nearest galaxy, Andromeda, two million light years away, we may wonder whether there are people there with even bigger telescopes looking at us. One of the most important questions that remains to be solved is whether there is life out there. It would be remarkable if the Earth were unique, the laboratory from which life can spread through the galaxy, giving it the most distinguished place in the cosmic scale. But we have no idea whether life is common or just an accident. The astronomer ought to react with equanimity to either prospect.

**19** What are the prospects for someone starting a career in astronomy today compared to 40 years ago?

   **A** Forty years ago, it was easy to discover something new.

   **B** The really crucial discovery about the universe has already been made.

   **C** Young astronomers are far better equipped nowadays.

   **D** It is essentially a young person's profession.

**20** What is the writer's attitude towards the possibility of there being life elsewhere in the universe?

   **A** It is the main reason for taking up the career.

   **B** It is a little frightening to think that others are observing us.

   **C** Earth is probably the centre from which life will develop elsewhere

   **D** It should not matter professionally whether we are alone or not.

## Are you ready to join a winning team?

We are looking for a top-class

### AUDITOR

to join our Group Internal Audit Department based in the South of England

Your role will be to report directly to the Head of the Group, to operate in a consultative capacity, and to liaise with senior management, with the primary aim of adding value and profitability to business operations.

### You will be expected to
- review the Group's systems development, infrastructure and operating environment.
- develop an annual plan to be presented to management.
- follow up progress made by implementing agreed action.

### Your Profile
You have a quality University Degree and are a qualified auditor. Ideally, you will also be a qualified chartered accountant with at least five years' previous experience, with a minimum of two years in Internal Audit. You are willing to travel. You are assertive, have exceptional analytical skill and can communicate your ideas readily. You have the ability to think and act at all times in a businesslike manner.

**21**  What is the main requirement of the job being advertised?
The successful candidate must

  **A**  take change of the auditing of the group.

  **B**  get on well with colleagues in a team.

  **C**  deal with the top management on equal terms.

  **D**  suggest ways in which the working of the group can be improved.

**22**  Which of these qualifications or abilities is not regarded as essential?

  **A**  five years' experience in the same kind of work

  **B**  willingness to travel

  **C**  the ability to impose one's personality

  **D**  the ability to explain things clearly

**Tip**

*Texts are sometimes presented in a different form, like this advertisement, but the approach is the same. Read through the text before looking at the questions.*

**Active Vocabulary List**

These are some words and phrases commonly connected with the subject of work. If you are not sure of the meaning of any words or phrases, look them up in your dictionary.

*work, job, employment
worker, employee, staff
employer, boss, manager
colleague, workmate*

*self-employed, freelance
at work, on duty, on/in business
hardworking, dedicated, overworked
monotony, boredom, strike*

**Professions**
*actor/actress, architect, author,
computer programmer, dentist,
doctor, engineer, film director,
journalist, lawyer, lecturer, scientist,
teacher, politician*

## Part 3 (Multiple-choice comprehension)

Read this article about a business in India. For questions **23**–**29**, choose the answer (**A**, **B**, **C** or **D**) which you think fits best according to the text.

### 19M POPPADOMS A DAY (AND RISING)

At 5.30 am the sun has not yet risen in Mumbai*. But in one small courtyard, a group of women is already at work. There's a clatter of metal buckets and the clank of weighing scales as the women start to mix dough. As the women chatter away there's a definite cottage industry feel about the proceedings. In reality, however, they are part of a mammoth all-female business that employs 40,000 people – and which, by the end of the same day, will have sold a staggering 19m poppadoms.

The courtyard is part of the Wadala branch of Shri Mahila Griha Udyog Lijjat Papad, a 'women's house industry' that is the world's largest poppadom provider. Most of India's breakfast, lunch and dinner tables are furnished with poppadoms from Lijjat, which has made itself the cornerstone of India's growing fast-food market. 'Housewives used to spend the entire month of May rolling poppadoms before the June monsoon came, when it would be too damp for them to dry,' says Irene Almeida, spokeswoman for the business. 'It was a tradition, But today, people just buy packets from us instead.' While exports to the US, the Gulf and the UK make up 10 per cent of the business, in India itself Lijjat is a household name.

But despite its scale, the business has a grassroots approach that fits the needs of its female workers. 'We all know each other,' says Prattibha, co-ordinator of the Wadala branch. 'It is like a family.' While the Wadala branch is full by first light, at 8 am the courtyard will be empty. Standing in a queue of sari-clad women, each holding a pile of poppadoms to be weighed, Sunanda explains: 'I come in the morning to pick up the dough. Then I go and roll the poppadoms at home in my own time. The next morning, I come back to get my poppadoms weighed, pick up my earnings, and take away some more dough balls.'

Lijjat was started by housewives who had their own needs at heart. One day a group of seven women who lived in one of Old Mumbai's dilapidated apartment blocks resolved to try to make poppadoms – known in India as papads – in their spare time. That was in 1959. Liqqat's tiny head office, on the fourth floor of the same ramshackle apartment block, is the only reminder of the small roots from which the business has grown. But the story of Liqqat's beginnings has taken on almost mythical proportions for Liqqat's women. After all, these are women whose lives have been transformed by their association with the business. 'Eighty per cent of women are illiterate and most are poor,' says Prattibha. 'Many have husbands who don't have jobs, who abuse drugs and alcohol, who beat their wives. Working for Lijjat gives the ladies a level of independence.' Prattibha even performs 'surprise' home visits, when she knows that one of her 'ladies' is suffering domestic violence.

Lijjat is not fussy about whom it employs, as long as they are capable of rolling dough into circles. 'If they live in a hut with no sunlight, or next to a gutter, they can come and work at one of the centres,' says Irene Almeida. Most are given two days' training, a teak rolling-pin and an aluminium rolling-board, and they are ready to start. 'As long as they agree to roll out a minimum of 3kg every day, they can come and go as they please.'

Granted the freedom to work as much or as little as they like, many women remain associated with Lijjat for decades. Every papad-roller is a part owner of the business and is called a sister member, with a right to vote on business policy. In fact, two years ago, the members were unhappy with the president of 14 years, and voted her out of office. Most talk passionately about the organisation. 'We are proud of being owners,' says one.

Liqqat's staff care is second to none. Every day a bus does the rounds, picking up women from different areas and bringing them to the centres. Most beneficial of all is the literacy programme for the women themselves, which started two years ago. In a small room at the Wadala branch, women sit on the floor, working their way through the alphabet. 'I know half the letters, although it has taken me nearly one year,' says an older woman named Saraswati Ghag. Even such a limited knowledge has brought improvements in Saraswati's life. 'I have got confidence now I know some letters.'

So far, 5,000 women have started the programme. 'My daughters can read and write properly,' says one of them, Sheela Waghamare. 'So they help me when they get home from school. They help me write letters to relatives that I haven't been in touch with for years.' Now Sheela and Saraswati can start to read Lijjat's monthly magazine, with its marriage announcements, its news of VIPs opening new branches, and its annual meeting reports.

Lijjat's logo reads 'Symbol of Women's Strength'. Every time any restaurant, hotel, shop or individual buys a packet of Lijjat papads they are reminded that this household name is a product of female endeavour. As Irene explains: 'People are made aware that women can run big businesses as well as men.'

---

* previously known as Bombay

*Article by Beatrice Newbery, © Financial Times Ltd*

23  What is unusual in the Indian context about the Lijjat organisation?

    **A**  It has developed from small beginnings.

    **B**  It is entirely staffed by women.

    **C**  It has such a large number of employees.

    **D**  It produces such a large quantity of poppadoms.

24  What is the main change that Lijjat has brought about in the market?

    **A**  Poppadoms are now exported.

    **B**  Housewives no longer make poppadoms at home.

    **C**  Poppadoms are available in the monsoon season.

    **D**  Most housewives now buy poppadoms ready made.

25  Why are the women in Paragraph 3 queuing at the Wadala branch?

    **A**  to buy poppadoms

    **B**  to collect dough

    **C**  to collect their earnings

    **D**  to register the work they have done

26  Why does Prattibha make 'surprise' visits to workers' homes? *(Paragraph 4)*

    **A**  to check up on the workers

    **B**  to check up on their husbands

    **C**  to inspect their living accommodation

    **D**  to ensure that they are paid

27  How does Lijjat differ from most other firms?

    **A**  It employs anyone able to do the work.

    **B**  It does not expect workers to have had previous experience.

    **C**  It only employs workers who are in need of money.

    **D**  It is not concerned that their homes may be dirty.

28  Which of these adjectives describes Lijjat's organisation most accurately?

    **A**  democratic

    **B**  revolutionary

    **C**  independent

    **D**  feminist

29  What is the greatest benefit of the literacy programme for Lijjat's workers?

    **A**  They can help their children with their studies.

    **B**  They do not lose contact with their families.

    **C**  They can read about the company's progress.

    **D**  They feel more self-sufficient.

## Part I

For questions 1–18, read the texts and decide which answer (**A**, **B**, **C** or **D**) best fits each gap.

### MILLENNIUM PERSON

Who was the most famous person of the last thousand years? *The Sunday Times* asked a number of historians this question, and the winner, by a wide (1) .............. , was Isaac Newton. But it was by no means a foregone (2) .............. . Panellists chose novelists, religious leaders, political theorists and psychologists. But most were in (3) .............. that a scientist should get the vote, though even here there was no (4) .............. of candidates. Newton could hardly have (5) .............. the Cambridge where he spent most of his working life as it is today, with the cars in the streets and the aircraft (6) .............. , but most scientists are of the opinion that we owe more to him and the crucial laws of physics he made known than to anyone else.

| | | | | | | | | | |
|---|---|---|---|---|---|---|---|---|---|
| 1 | **A** | score | **B** | margin | **C** | difference | **D** | range |
| 2 | **A** | decision | **B** | result | **C** | response | **D** | conclusion |
| 3 | **A** | agreement | **B** | acceptance | **C** | consent | **D** | coincidence |
| 4 | **A** | absence | **B** | shortage | **C** | drought | **D** | default |
| 5 | **A** | previewed | **B** | advertised | **C** | foreseen | **D** | promoted |
| 6 | **A** | above | **B** | upward | **C** | on top | **D** | overhead |

### THE MAN WHO MADE SENSE OUT OF ROCKS

In 1792 a young engineer, William Smith, went down a coal mine. At that time no one knew why minerals were found in different parts of the country. But Smith was very (7) .............. , and made notes of what he saw. He saw that coal (8) .............. in layers within other layers of rock and the layers (9) .............. downwards. This (10) .............. him to the conclusion that if rocks had fossils, the plants and animals (11) .............. in a layer would identify that strata. Smith eventually completed a map of the strata of England, which is the basis of modern geology. It was an extraordinary achievement for a man, working unaided and (12) .............. a sick wife, which fortunately, towards the end of his life, brought him fame and fortune.

| | | | | | | | | | |
|---|---|---|---|---|---|---|---|---|---|
| 7 | **A** | observant | **B** | vigilant | **C** | alert | **D** | watchful |
| 8 | **A** | grew | **B** | materialised | **C** | took place | **D** | occurred |
| 9 | **A** | inclined | **B** | sloped | **C** | slipped | **D** | slanted |
| 10 | **A** | directed | **B** | indicated | **C** | led | **D** | took |
| 11 | **A** | kept | **B** | stocked | **C** | maintained | **D** | preserved |
| 12 | **A** | caring | **B** | nursing | **C** | minding | **D** | attending |

### HISTORY AS FACT OR FICTION

The history books of my childhood were full of popular myths – how the Saxon hero, King Alfred, burnt the cakes, how Sir Francis Drake was playing bowls when the Spanish Armada (13) .............. into sight and insisted on finishing the game. Strangely enough, there may be (14) .............. of truth in the latter story. But the myths themselves, true or not, are (15) ............. to revision.  Richard III is a villain in Shakespeare's play because the Tudor family, who succeeded him, (16) ............... him of the murder of his young nephews, justifying their own claim to the throne. Modern research suggests that the Tudor, Henry VII, not Richard, was probably (17) .............. of the murder,  so Richard's reputation has been (18) ............... .

| 13 | **A** appeared | **B** showed | **C** arrived | **D** came |
|----|---------------|--------------|---------------|------------|
| 14 | **A** an element | **B** an ingredient | **C** a component | **D** a part |
| 15 | **A** liable | **B** apt | **C** subject | **D** inclined |
| 16 | **A** accused | **B** blamed | **C** charged | **D** demanded |
| 17 | **A** responsible | **B** guilty | **C** to blame | **D** at fault |
| 18 | **A** recovered | **B** resumed | **C** recuperated | **D** rehabilitated |

### Vocabulary Development

Complete the sentences below with a word or phrase taken from the choices for the questions you have answered. The sentences are printed in the same order as the questions. Note the difference between the correct answer below and a phrase of similar meaning in the passages above.

1   The contract was terminated by mutual ................................... .

2   It was a remarkable ................................... that we were both in Lithuania at that time.

3   There has been no rain for months, and many areas are affected by ................................... .

4   An enormous lorry suddenly ................................... out of the fog in front of us.

5   Rays of sunlight ................................... down diagonally towards the beach.

6   The evidence ................................... that all rocks follow the same pattern.

7   Smith undertook the work while ................................... for his sick wife.

8   He ................................... the other driver for the accident.

9   He was arrested and ................................... with murder.

10  He had a heavy fall, and it was some time before he ................................... consciousness.

## Part 2

These two texts are concerned with different aspects of ancient history.  For questions **19–22**, choose the answer (**A**, **B**, **C** or **D**) which you think fits best according to the text.

### THE ORIGIN OF THE MEDITERRANEAN

To the Greeks and early Romans, there was no Mediterranean. It was simply 'the sea'. For a long time there were no others. The Pillars of Hercules, near modern Cadiz in Spain, marked the limits of the known world. People visited them, largely so that they could boast of having been there, to the very edge. Beyond, there was simply the great encircling river, the Ocean.

The conquest of Britain changed the perspective to a certain extent, though nearly 200 years passed before a Roman geographer thought that he had better include it and started referring to the Mediterranean as the Inland Sea. The name Mediterranean (middle of the Earth) derived from its place in the Roman world, which stretched from Britain to North Africa. But what was, and still is, apparent is that it is almost enclosed. Until the Suez Canal was built, there was only one way out, and even now the two exits are narrow and historically it has been very important to hold the keys that let others in and out.

19    In ancient times, the Pillars of Hercules were of interest as

    **A**    the gateway to Britain.

    **B**    the only way of reaching the Atlantic.

    **C**    a kind of tourist resort.

    **D**    the basis for the name of the sea.

20    The name Mediterranean was given to the sea because it seemed

    **A**    inland.

    **B**    central.

    **C**    enclosed.

    **D**    narrow.

## WHAT WE OWE TO THE ANCIENT GREEKS

After nearly 2,500 years, the golden age of 5th century BC Athens still plays a vital part in the consciousness of every European. Dramatists return over and over again to the myths for their subjects. Even guided missiles carry the names of Greek gods. The word most often quoted by our politicians as desirable is Greek – democracy.

The golden age of Ancient Greece is not universally admired. Multiculturalists object to its exclusion of foreigners as 'barbarians'; feminists decry the situation of women. But its appeal is sustained by the variety of interpretations available. We take from it what suits our own convictions, and so Pericles was a freedom-fighter or an imperialist, depending on one's point of view.

But perhaps the most enduring legacy that it has left us is to be found in the drama of Euripides, even though contemporaries were critical of his treatment of the myths. There we can recognise ourselves, striving to be rational and make sense of the suffering in the world, but incapable of controlling our emotions or doing very much to change it.

**21**  Why does the writer think that Ancient Greece is still important in our society?

    **A**  It is our ideal of society.

    **B**  It provides us with a set of names that everyone recognises.

    **C**  It is the basis of modern political thought.

    **D**  It can act as a model, whatever opinions we hold.

**22**  What is the writer saying about the relevance of Euripides' drama to us?

    **A**  Like much of our drama, it was revolutionary.

    **B**  It interests us because the gods are presented with human attitudes.

    **C**  It is recognisable as a reflection of the human situation today.

    **D**  It demonstrates that most great art is not appreciated in its own time.

**Active Vocabulary List**

These are some words and phrases commonly connected with the subject of history. If you are not sure of the meaning of any words or phrases, look them up in your dictionary.

| | |
|---|---|
| history, the past | historic – not the same as historical |
| date, sixteenth century | event, war, battle, invasion |
| discovery, invention, achievement | leader, dictator, revolutionary |
| Prime Minister, cabinet, minister | king, queen, emperor, empress |
| aristocracy, nobles, parliament | democracy, election, vote, referendum |

## Part 3 (Ordering paragraphs)

This article consists of 15 paragraphs. Seven of them have been removed. Choose from the paragraphs **A-H** the one that fits each gap (**23-29**). There is one extra paragraph that does not fit and which you do not need to use.

### IT'S QUEEN VICTORIA, BUT NOT AS WE KNOW HER

Queen Victoria lived her life like a butterfly in reverse. She began as a gay young thing, flitting from party to party, a fashion-loving dance addict, of whom it was said: 'She never saw dawn but through a ballroom window.' Then, abruptly widowed at 42, she crawled into a cocoon of mourning. So long did Victoria spend stitched up in her widow's weeds that part of her life has come to stand for the whole. In the popular imagination, she is like a black hole from which only one idea has escaped: that she was not amused.

**23** _____

This Victoria is one who could easily have grown into the heroine of the 1997 film of her relationship with her Scottish servant, Brown. But whereas that was an intriguing account of a spirited old monarch who always wanted a man in her life, this is about the sexy young queen, played by 30-year-old Victoria Hamilton. When the production was first announced, the producer, David Cunliffe, called Victoria and Albert 'a lusty couple', and this statement, plus the programme-makers' proposal to dramatise the intimacy of the couple's wedding night, caused a right royal fuss.

**24** _____

One biographer has even said the couple's bedroom was full of nude statues, and they had a device that meant they could lock the door without getting out of bed. 'Albert was interested in anything mechanical, and they were among the first people to have a lift installed, so it wouldn't surprise me,' says Cunliffe. 'You only have to look at the catalogue of Osbourne, their house on the Isle of Wight, to see the statues they had, though all very tasteful, of course.'

**25** _____

But from a political point of view, what we'll see is only a taste of what might have been. If the BBC hadn't lost its nerve, says Cunliffe, the two-part series would have run and run. Originally, six parts were planned, taking the queen from cradle to grave. But it would have meant spending with as much profligacy as the royal family itself, and, as the writer, John Goldsmith, explains: 'The story was too complicated, with too many children, grandchildren

and great-grandchildren, too many prime ministers, too many wars.' So it was decided to focus on the single narrative strand of the love story, enlivened by politics.

**26** _____

Because, for all her steeliness, Victoria didn't really have a clue. 'The beginning of the reign was little short of a disaster,' says the historian David Starkey. 'She was guilty of complete constitutional impropriety, and her whole relationship with Melbourne, the prime minister, was disgraceful because she was so outrageously partisan. The constitutional monarchy was only just being invented. The first king to say it was his duty to suppress his private wishes in favour of his duties to the commonwealth was William IV, whom Victoria succeeded.'

**27** _____

History hasn't been kind to him. 'The English have always treated foreign rulers badly,' says Starkey. 'At the time, the English loathed Albert.' It didn't help that he was cripplingly shy and hopeless in public. He was also a good deal more easily shocked than his wife. A figure of immense rectitude and correctness, he was furious to discover Lord Uxbridge was keeping his mistress in the palace, while Victoria didn't turn a hair.

**28** _____

Cunliffe agrees. 'They brought him up badly. Victoria wasn't a good mother, either, but women weren't allowed to be, in many ways. They gave birth, but then they saw their children only intermittently, when they were clean.'

**29** _____

Which is what Starkey will be doing next month. Royal history doesn't get more personal than the way Henry VIII's love life affected church and state, and Starkey has made a documentary series about the king's wives for Channel 4. So perhaps Victoria and Albert will set a new trend. Our sometimes monstrous, sometimes brilliant royal families are a source of great tales. Surely the butterfly queen would have been amused.

*Article by Sally Kinnes, © The Sunday Times*

**A** Fortunately for her, Albert was an astute politician and he ended up running the show. His correspondence makes clear that eventually he was acting as a cross between the monarch and the prime minister. Even more than the vivacious Victoria of the series, it is Albert who is the revelation.

**B** In fact, the intriguing thing is how much further the drama could have gone. 'We know from her diaries and her letters that her wedding night was 'wonderful – a taste of heaven', says Cunliffe. 'My belief is that she was very warm-blooded and passionate.'

**C** It is said that until the 1930s the palace refused permission for any drama about Victoria and even when two laudatory films were made, with Anna Neagle as the queen, helping to restore the royal family's reputation after the abdication of Edward VIII in 1936, Victoria's three surviving children, all very old ladies, had to give their personal approval of the choice of actress.

**D** BBC1's new two part drama, *Victoria and Albert*, changes all that. It concentrates on the butterfly years. Like a Hollywood weepie, it takes this relationship between first cousins and traces its transformation from cool indifference and what was more or less a marriage of convenience into one of the great love stories of the 19th century.

**E** As the series underlines, at the outset Albert was incredibly bright, but Victoria was queen. This disparity meant, to begin with at least, that he had nothing to do. 'It seems that there were contemporary resonances,' says Goldsmith, 'It is the woman who is more powerful and rich and important, and that's increasingly a phenomenon today. Albert was like a puppy dog, walking two paces behind.' The rows between the couple shook the palace.

**F** Bertie, Victoria's eldest son, felt the pressure of his father's disapproval. Although Albert was affectionate and played games with his children, he had enormous expectations, and Bertie crumbled when he was unable to live up to them. 'Albert had a highly developed view of an intensive educational programme,' says Starkey, 'which is no use if you've got a thick son. Bertie wasn't academic, though he had what we might call emotional intelligence.'

**G** A hundred years after her death, Victoria still fascinates, and not only because of what we can reconstruct of her love life. By Cunliffe's reckoning, there have been more books written about her than anyone else in England. But given the life she led, it's no surprise. Even her accession was a fraught affair, and from the outset, her mother was pitched against the uncle she succeeded, William IV.

**H** But the clash of personalities makes for great drama. The first part of the series is so engaging that you wonder why television doesn't tackle royal history more often. Simon Schama has done it with his acclaimed *History of Britain*, effectively a series of mini-narratives, centred on the monarch. Starkey agrees with Schama: 'Personal history has got it right, and academic history has got it wrong. We should take the personalities seriously.'

**Tip**

*How are you getting on with this kind of text? If you didn't do very well last time, look at the guidance given once again. Try to develop an eye for clues. In this text many names are mentioned. Bear in mind that most students get this kind of test almost all right or almost all wrong. If you get it right it counts for 20% of all the marks you need.*

## Part I

For questions 1–18, read the texts and decide which answer (**A**, **B**, **C** or **D**) best fits each gap.

---

**WHY SOME OF US ARE ABSENT-MINDED**

Are you liable to (1) ............... the bathroom with water because you forget to (2) ............... the tap? Do you miss business appointments or lose your way on simple journeys? If so, there's a chance that it is not your (3) ............... . Recent research has (4) ............... a rare condition resulting from oxygen starvation at birth that is responsible in many of such cases.

The condition went unrecognised until now because, (5) ............... the handicap, sufferers usually perform quite well at school. The problem is only likely to become severe in later life when the damage caused to the (6) ............... memory might make it difficult for adults to lead independent lives.

---

| 1 | A | deluge | B | flood | C | overflow | D | splash |
|---|---|--------|---|-------|---|----------|---|--------|
| 2 | A | cut off | B | cut out | C | turn off | D | turn out |
| 3 | A | blame | B | fault | C | guilt | D | mistake |
| 4 | A | identified | B | classified | C | signified | D | typified |
| 5 | A | although | B | despite | C | in spite | D | nevertheless |
| 6 | A | long-run | B | long-span | C | long-term | D | long-time |

---

**ONE MAN'S ART COLLECTION**

Many years ago, Gustav Rau inherited a factory. He sold it, trained as a doctor and (7) ............... a lifetime building hospitals in Africa. But at the same time, he quietly (8) ............... together the second largest private art collection in the world.

Dr Rau might have remained out of the public (9) ............... if he had not retired to Monaco and been found wandering (10) ............... through the streets. A Swiss court declared him mentally incapable and the authorities (11) ............... the collection. But Dr Rau's mind (12) ............... not to be impaired; he made a will, leaving his collection to UNICEF, and the paintings are now in Germany.

---

| 7 | A | passed | B | gave | C | consumed | D | spent |
|---|---|--------|---|------|---|----------|---|-------|
| 8 | A | compiled | B | lumped | C | put | D | stored |
| 9 | A | eye | B | sight | C | view | D | vision |
| 10 | A | accidentally | B | aimlessly | C | emptily | D | irregularly |
| 11 | A | took in | B | took out | C | took over | D | took up |
| 12 | A | came about | B | resulted | C | succeeded | D | turned out |

### THE RETURN OF THE HOLLYWOOD EPIC

In the 1950s, when television was beginning to threaten the film industry, Hollywood looked to ancient Rome for its reply. Epics like *Ben Hur* and *Spartacus* made immense (13) .............. . But the catastrophic failure of *Cleopatra* turned them into a synonym for disaster.

So the producers of *Gladiator* were running a huge (14) .............. in reviving the genre, and without their consistent (15) .............. record of box-office successes, the film might not have been made. It was a shrewd decision to (16) .............. most of the leading roles to British actors, respecting the convention that the Romans did not speak American English, and for the star part of the *Gladiator*, a New Zealander who was something of an (17) .............. quantity was preferred to more established names. The rest, as they say, is history. The gamble (18) .............. and audiences all over the world flocked to see a Roman epic once again.

| 13 | A | benefits | B | gains | C | profits | D | rewards |
|----|---|----------|---|-------|---|---------|---|---------|
| 14 | A | chance | B | hazard | C | risk | D | speculation |
| 15 | A | track | B | path | C | course | D | trail |
| 16 | A | convey | B | confer | C | bequeath | D | entrust |
| 17 | A | inexperienced | B | ignorant | C | uncertain | D | unknown |
| 18 | A | paid back | B | paid off | C | paid out | D | paid up |

**Tip**

*You have one hour 30 minutes to complete the whole test. Do not spend too long on any one part, and remember that questions 1-18 are worth one mark, questions 19-40 are worth two!*

## Part 2

You are going to read four extracts on different topics. For questions **19–26**, choose the answer (**A, B, C** or **D**) which you think fits best according to the text.

---

### SO WHAT HAPPENED TO THE ENGLISH LANGUAGE?

Anyone who wants to learn or use what used to be called 'plain English' is likely to be disheartened by what has been happening in recent years. In the first place, there has been the proliferation of jargon – terminology devised by the experts to ensure that only they will grasp what is being said. Its use is of great value to academics, lawyers and economists since the ordinary citizen is obliged to consult them, usually for a substantial fee, to find out what they mean.

Far more sinister is the perversion of everyday terms to mean something quite different. This is favoured by those who regard themselves as 'politically correct' – a term that, by implying that only they know what is right, is itself a perversion of language. No doubt it started off with good intentions. It was only natural that the original inhabitants of North America should object to what they were called, since they are neither 'red' nor 'Indian', but it is doubtful whether they appreciated being renamed as the predecessors of an obscure Italian navigator*. But in their anxiety not to offend anyone, these 'idealists' are making nonsense of the language. Those who are short of stature may feel happier to be described as 'vertically challenged' but what comfort does it offer the very tall, like myself, who feel 'vertically challenged' every time we bang our heads?

\* *'America' is derived from Amerigo Vespucci, thought at the time to have been the first European to have set foot on the continent.*

---

**19**  What is the writer saying in the first paragraph about jargon?

**A**  It is devised to put people off learning the language.

**B**  It excludes the majority of people from comprehension.

**C**  It is only used by professionally qualified people.

**D**  They employ it as a way of increasing their income.

**20**  Which of these terms in inverted commas is the writer using ironically?

**A**  'plain English'

**B**  'politically correct'

**C**  'idealists'

**D**  'vertically challenged'

### WHERE PANTOMIME IS STILL THE SAME

The Players' Theatre, near Charing Cross Station in London, is the only one left in the country where pantomime is still performed in the traditional manner at Christmas. The theatre is an odd institution, a club whose members are dedicated to keeping alive the spirit of the Victorian music hall. When the MC (or Master of Ceremonies), as he is traditionally called, says the century is coming to an end, he means the 19th; when he proposes the health of the Queen, he means Victoria, not Elizabeth. For the MC, modern pantomime is a disgusting spectacle, a distortion of a great tradition. The comedians make jokes about topical events to amuse the adults, while the children, who go wanting to follow a story, are bored and don't understand.

The old forms are not quite dead, however; nor were Victorian pantomimes so far removed from the present day. A well-known comedian who has written four shows for different theatres points out that pantomime was in decline until popular music-hall stars began to take part. In his opinion, since television is the modern equivalent of music hall, it is only natural that jokes should refer to soap opera. There must still be a connection with the original stories; if they are abandoned, how can the name of pantomime be retained? But like all art forms, it must move with the times; a strict attention to the original forms would mean empty seats and limit its appeal to a few enthusiasts.

21    What point is the writer making about the Players' Theatre in the first paragraph?
    **A**  It is unique.
    **B**  It is strange.
    **C**  It is exclusive.
    **D**  It is out of date.

22    What point is the comedian making that contradicts the MC's statement?
    **A**  Pantomime was kept alive by the kind of actors who star today.
    **B**  Jokes about TV programmes are the main attraction for the audience.
    **C**  There is no need to repeat the same stories all the time.
    **D**  No one has any respect for the tradition nowadays.

## LONDON THEATRES

### ADELPHI

*Chicago*

Winner! Outstanding musical!
Kill for a ticket.

### ALBERY

*Private Lives*

Subtle revival of Noel Coward's
masterpiece

### COMEDY

*The Homecoming*

Pinter's scary, stunning play
Don't dare miss it!

### DUCHESS

*Blue/Orange*

Most thrilling play in town
Shockingly good cast

### FORTUNE

*The Woman In Black*

13th spine-chilling year
The audience screamed.

### GIELGUD

*The Graduate*

Linda Gray is the Mrs Robinson
we've been waiting for.

### HAYMARKET

*The Royal Family*

Judi Dench returns to the
stage like an empress.

### WYNDHAMS

*The Play What I Wrote*

Directed by Kenneth Branagh
with surprise celebrity guest

---

23    In which theatre is the leading role now taken by a different actress?

    **A**  Albery

    **B**  Gielgud

    **C**  Haymarket

    **D**  Wyndhams

24    Which theatre would you go to if you enjoy being frightened?

    **A**  Adelphi

    **B**  Comedy

    **C**  Duchess

    **D**  Fortune

**WHAT DO BUSINESSWOMEN REALLY WANT?**

An index to women in business reveals that almost half of the largest 100 companies have no women on their boards and it is a dispiriting sign that they still feel the need to get together at meetings to work out their strategies for breaking through. One such meeting in London recently suggested that the obstacle holding British women back is cultural. British women, unlike their American counterparts, were seen as demure and modest, the result of their upbringing. In consequence, they tended to communicate in a roundabout manner, asking for opinions instead of putting themselves forward. While consultation is of value, it can be seen as a sign of weakness and insecurity.

A survey of high-flying women nevertheless indicated that they have different targets from men. Nearly all of them, as compared with hardly any of the corresponding sample of men interviewed, regarded personal fulfilment as the factor that most influenced their choice of career, while men were more likely to take salary into account. The majority of women sought a satisfying job in agreeable surroundings and empire building, the necessary preliminary for reaching the top, did not appeal to them. For this reason, and in some cases because they are obliged to put the family first and the company second, women are still few and far between in the corridors of power.

25   What is the writer saying about British businesswomen in the first paragraph?
    **A**   They have given up hope because there are so few of them at the top.
    **B**   They feel that they will never succeed unless they all work together.
    **C**   Their education has discouraged self-assertion.
    **D**   They do not know their own minds, like American women.

26   What does the writer imply is the main difference in motivation between men and women which accounts for men being more likely to be in positions of authority?
    **A**   Men are primarily motivated by money.
    **B**   Women do not have as much desire for power and influence.
    **C**   Job satisfaction is all that matters to women.
    **D**   Women have responsibilities towards the family.

## Part 3

This article consists of 15 paragraphs. Seven of them have been removed. Choose from the paragraphs **A–H** the one that fits each gap (**27–33**). There is one extra paragraph that does not fit and which you do not need to use.

### SO OFF SHE WENT TO THE CIRCUS

The circus performer Nell Gifford's winter quarters are just off the A417 to Cheltenham. At first glance, it's a typical English rural scene – corrugated iron barns and rickety outhouses, bits of machinery, gas canisters, a rash of abandoned-looking vehicles, humming traffic noise, an Alsatian and, towering above it all, five huge black grain silos.

| 27 |

Nell Gifford appears in her riding costume. For a 28-year-old, Gifford has accomplished a lot. She has taken a degree in English at Oxford, worked her way up from circus groom to ringmistress, written a successful book about her apprenticeship, and today runs her own circus, in which she performs on Perlo, her beautiful pony. For all that, though, she has a dreamy, distracted air.

| 28 |

Gifford disappears behind a curtain and reappears in a short skirt. Her knees are covered in scars. 'I got quite badly kicked in a show. I had to canter round the outside of the ring and there was a horse in the middle turning and it just lashed out and kicked me really hard across the knee. But you have to keep looking at the public and smiling. I was just trying to keep going but it was so, so painful.'

| 29 |

She hands me a small, red programme. The introduction starts by describing how, ever since she was 18, she had dreamt of having her own circus, and how, when she was 25 and about to join the prestigious Roncalli Circus in Germany, she had fallen in love with Toti Gifford, a landscape gardener who was storing some tools on the farm where she kept her caravan. A year later, they were married. With some of their friends, they started to build up the circus. They built caravans, renovated some old fairground games and gradually built up a team of craftsmen and artists.

| 30 |

But how did this spectacle begin? Nell was born in Oxford. When she was ten, her parents moved to a village in Gloucestershire. The family lived in a large country house. It was a privileged upbringing. Nell and Clover had ponies. 'We were lucky,' Nell says. 'We were blessed with a really happy childhood. My mum just made it really idyllic.'

| 31 |

For two years, she sat in the box office every morning and when trade was quiet, wrote her book, *Josser.* It is in part an elegy to the circus, the glitter and romance of the big top, and the extraordinary discipline and dedication of the great performers. But it is also in part a 'down and out' autobiography, recording the long hours, the sleepless nights when the circus was being moved. Gifford says that, had it not been for her mother's accident, she would never have developed the resilience to stand the 'really grim bits' of her early days in the circus.

| 32 |

This year it is a little easier. Gifford says she is pretty sure that she will break even and even make a small profit. Yet there have been problems. Because of the outbreak of foot-and-mouth disease, the Giffords had to cancel all their bookings for three months. They also had to abandon the idea of introducing goats into their show.

| 33 |

It is a fine sight – the green field, the pony trotting and Gifford, with her long, tangled, golden hair reaching out behind her. The reality is slightly less picturesque. Gifford wants the pony to run to find out if, as she suspects, he is slightly lame. Afterwards, she picks up one of Perlo's front legs and finds a slight swelling on the hoof.

*Article by Amanda Mitchison © Telegraph Group Limited*

**A** There is a pause. And then she adds, a little dismissively: 'Oh, and I was savaged by a horse in Germany. A little stallion bit me all round the neck. But, apart from that – well, none of them are permanent injuries.'

**B** But what do other circus people, the real circus people who have been born into it, say about her and her show? Gifford laughs: 'They say it reminds them of when they were young. This is what they grew up with.'

**C** And yet, things are not so bleak as they might appear. There is a space between the performers' caravans where they can sit out, with a magnificent armchair. A closer inspection reveals that there is a certain antiquarian style to the junk: an ornate old sewing machine, for example. There are no crisp packets, no old curling plastic to be seen.

**D** There are still some 'grim bits' today. Toti's other job as a landscape gardener has thus far bankrolled the business but even so, things have been tight. Gifford points to one of the caravans. 'Last year we couldn't afford to put wheels on the wagons. We were so close to the line.'

**E** Ideas were plundered from any number of sources. For designs, Gifford looked at old children's books and sewing patterns. She and Toti saw a picture of a man with a violin on a trapeze wire and this was incorporated into the clown's act. The show has its own distinctive style and is accompanied by two musicians. The acts, presided over by Toti, the ringmaster, include a singing trapeze artist, a juggler, tap dancers, and of course, Nell Gifford, with her long hair floating as she rides around the ring with Perlo.

**F** The caravan that she shares with her husband, Toti, feels like the inside of a ship's cabin. Gifford takes off her boots. Her jacket, bought by her younger sister, Clover, in a job lot at an auction, belongs to another era. In Gifford's Circus, most things – the caravans, the hand-painted lettering on the billboards, the hand-turned children's roundabout – have a 1930s feel about them.

**G** But Gifford's pony, Perlo, remains. He is out to grass in a meadow and after the interview we go to see him. Gifford goes over to him. The pony is neatly built with a handsome face. She gives him an apple and a few affectionate claps on the neck. Then she turns him across the field, urging him to go faster.

**H** The idyll came to a sudden end. In 1991, when Nell was 18, her mother Charlotte was injured in a riding accident and suffered catastrophic brain damage. Today she cannot speak. She is cared for in a nursing home. After the accident, Nell went and worked in an American circus for a month and was smitten by the experience. Three years later, when she had finished her university degree, she went looking for a job in the circus. She started at the bottom, as box-office attendant. Then she changed circuses and got a job as a groom. Eventually, having moved circuses again, she began work as a ringmistress and bought a horse.

## Part 4

Read this article about modern architecture. For questions **34–40**, choose the answer (**A**, **B**, **C** or **D**) which you think fits best according to the text.

### SHOW ON THE ROAD

There are moments when you realise that the entire national consciousness has shifted slightly. Why? Because something happens that would previously have been insanely impossible, but now passes almost without comment. Take, for example, the newly completed London headquarters of the fashion retailer, Monsoon. Another glittering high-tech business park building? No way. This is real, full-blooded, original 1960s architecture, brought back from the dead. And it sings.

We've known for a while that some previously hated 1960s concrete architecture was coming to be regarded with affection, especially by the cognoscenti. But Monsoon shows that 'historic' modernist architecture can now command reverence bordering on awe. This successful company could have moved anywhere it wanted. And it did, but not the way you'd expect. It chose to buy, restore and convert the derelict, long-abandoned Paddington maintenance depot, which looms over the elevated urban motorway of the Westway like an ocean liner.

The result is electrifying. This was a building designed in the early 1960s, with the then unbuilt motorway in mind. It's in love with the motorway; one

26 curving wing slides underneath it, another virtually
27 kisses it. At its prow are two heroic funnels. It is set on a rising bend in the road, from which it seems to
29 be sailing towards you, on a collision course. It would be inconceivable for such a building to be built today. It would not be allowed to come so close to vehicles that, from inside, you can make eye contact with the drivers. The staff restaurant is right by the road. It's called, with dark humour, Bangers and Crash.

The building's original architect was Paul Hamilton, of the practice Bicknell and Hamilton. Today it has been rejuvenated by a new generation, notably Ceri Davies, of Allford Hall Monaghan Morris. Some of their own work harks back to this period. But here they have dealt with a real, glorious period one-off.

Hamilton, who's still around, aged 77, somehow managed to make an exceptional building from a dull brief in incredibly constrained surroundings. He was given a patch of land left over from the swirl of proposed motorway and roads. This patch happened to be on the far side of the motorway from the railway goods yard it was intended to serve, though it was linked up beneath the elevated road. On the southern motorway/goods yard side, all is industrial desolation. The goods yard, its railway lines long gone, is now part of the vast, frenzied construction site surrounding Paddington. But on the northern side, with that abrupt change of scale, pace and texture at which London excels, you are immediately in a different world. This is the leafy world of Little Venice, where canals flow between trees, where stuccoed villas abound, where people sip frothy lattes at open-air cafés. Hamilton's building mediates between the two worlds.

He was in his thirties when the commission came in. So, in architectural terms, it's a young man's building. He relates how it took just four weeks from getting the commission to getting planning permission. Moreover, he had a totally free hand. 'The budget was left to me,' he recalls. 'I knew it would get no maintenance, so I designed it to last. Everyone agreed they would take my word for it.

And today? Davies and her colleagues have made some fairly hefty alterations. They have inserted a mezzanine floor on the ground level, where the parcel trucks used to drive in and out, and added some new windows. But the only parts of the building that had decayed to the point of needing replacement were the bands of projecting metal-framed windows.

For new items such as the main reception desk and the moveable furniture in the staff restaurant, Davies has kept in touch with the curved lines of the original building. Fortunately, Monsoon, which employs about 200 designers, pattern-cutters and office staff, is an open-plan organisation, so there was little need to divide up the spaces. The interior is clearly of 2001 rather than of 35 years ago – pastiche is avoided – but it is sympathetic to the architecture.

There have been some losses. But you have to bear in mind that only a few years back it was all slated for demolition. Monsoon has shown imagination and no little courage in taking the place on at all, spending about £10 million to convert it when many another such organisation would merely have rented an existing block.

Such buildings, when they are out of fashion, are strangely invisible. Brought back to life for a new use, they suddenly become landmarks. Nobody paid the old Bankside power station much heed until it became the Tate Modern art gallery. In its very different way, this other industrial building has now emerged from its long sleep. It looks absolutely fresh.

*Article by Hugh Pearman © The Sunday Times*

**34** In what way does the Monsoon building illustrate what the writer says in the first sentence?

A  What one generation is against, the next is bound to admire.

B  People accept as normal something they used to think was absurd.

C  Once the experts recognise the value of something, others gradually come round to the same point of view.

D  Nowadays companies often prefer to take over old buildings rather than rent new ones.

**35** Which of these words in the third paragraph does not continue the writer's image of the building as being like 'an ocean liner'?

A  wing *(line 26)*

B  prow *(line 27)*

C  funnels *(line 27)*

D  sailing *(line 29)*

**36** What was the point of the joke changing the name of the staff restaurant from Bangers and Mash (sausages and mashed potatoes)?

A  There had been a number of accidents nearby.

B  Diners can watch car drivers going by.

C  Drivers may crash, surprised to see people eating near them.

D  If cars go off the road, they may come into the restaurant.

**37** What is the writer saying in paragraph 5 about the building and its surroundings?

A  The architect was given a very uninteresting job to do.

B  Unfortunately, he had to build on the less attractive side of the road.

C  The building would have fitted in better further north.

D  The building seems to bridge the contrast between industry and art.

**38** What is the architect's explanation for the way he was treated?

A  People let him have his own way because he was young.

B  Architects were not subject to any controls in those days.

C  Everyone trusted him to do a good job.

D  Everyone accepted that he was honest.

**39** How does the interior of the new office block relate to the original building?

A  It has been carefully designed to imitate its shape.

B  It contrasts with it because people do not have separate offices.

C  It is modern but blends well with the architecture.

D  It may be necessary to divide the building in two.

**40** What is the writer saying in the last two paragraphs about buildings like this?

A  It is a risky business to spend money on them.

B  They are transformed by the purpose they are used for.

C  We take notice of them again when they are used differently.

D  They become attractive when they are used as the architect intended.

# *Crime and the law*

For questions 1–18, read the texts and decide which answer (**A**, **B**, **C** or **D**) best fits each gap.

## FALSE ALARM?

Have you ever passed a shop, obviously closed, seen a red light (1) ............... on and off and heard an alarm sounding? Almost certainly you did nothing about it. It never occurred to you to (2) ............... the police because you took it for (3) ............... that it was a false alarm. In nine cases out of ten you would have been right.

If you hear a neighbour's alarm you may feel under a certain (4) ............... to investigate, but the (5) ............... of false alarms to genuine ones is very similar; it is far too easy for the alarm to be (6) ............... by a cat or a dog, left alone in the house.

As a result, any new systems installed must now carry further detectors to indicate whether the alarm is false.

| | | | | | | | | |
|---|---|---|---|---|---|---|---|---|
| 1 | **A** | shining | **B** | flashing | **C** | glowing | **D** | sparkling |
| 2 | **A** | alert | **B** | alarm | **C** | signal | **D** | communicate |
| 3 | **A** | certain | **B** | sure | **C** | definite | **D** | granted |
| 4 | **A** | duty | **B** | obligation | **C** | liability | **D** | responsibility |
| 5 | **A** | scale | **B** | balance | **C** | ratio | **D** | degree |
| 6 | **A** | touched on | **B** | set off | **C** | started out | **D** | opened up |

## DARING ROBBERY PREVENTED

Six men went on (7) ............... yesterday for having planned what would have been the world's biggest robbery, involving diamonds worth £200 million pounds (8) ............... last year in the Millennium Dome. The gang, who were driving a vehicle specially adapted to their purpose, were (9) ............... by an undercover police operation. The robbery was professionally organised and the thieves would probably have got (10) ............... it if the police had not kept them under (11) ............... . When the raid took place, four of the six were caught red-handed, and two more were (12) ............... later.

| | | | | | | | | |
|---|---|---|---|---|---|---|---|---|
| 7 | **A** | charge | **B** | court | **C** | process | **D** | trial |
| 8 | **A** | in exhibition | **B** | in show | **C** | on display | **D** | on parade |
| 9 | **A** | avoided | **B** | evaded | **C** | foiled | **D** | resisted |
| 10 | **A** | away with | **B** | on with | **C** | off with | **D** | out with |
| 11 | **A** | inspection | **B** | observation | **C** | examination | **D** | watch |
| 12 | **A** | detained | **B** | retained | **C** | confined | **D** | restricted |

## SHOPLIFTING

Stealing from shops does not (13) .............. very high in the category of serious crime and because it (14) .............. involves violence, the police treat it as low priority. Yet for gangs of criminals it is big (15) .............. , above all because the courts are (16) .............. towards offenders. Most of them, even when caught and convicted, are merely cautioned and (17) .............. free with a warning.

In a typical case, the police officer may spend hours taking down (18) .............. from the person accused. The sentence is a fine that does not cover the cost of the goods stolen. Firms wonder whether it is worth the trouble of reporting the theft.

| | | | | | | | | |
|----|---|----------------|---|-------------|---|--------------|---|--------------|
| 13 | A | class | B | grade | C | rank | D | count |
| 14 | A | infrequently | B | rarely | C | unusually | D | uncommonly |
| 15 | A | business | B | commerce | C | trade | D | industry |
| 16 | A | patient | B | lenient | C | disposed | D | tender |
| 17 | A | let | B | made | C | set | D | released |
| 18 | A | a claim | B | an allegation | C | an expression | D | a statement |

## Vocabulary Development

Complete the sentences below with a word or phrase taken from the choices for the questions you have answered. The sentences are printed in the same order as the questions. Note the difference between the correct answer below and a phrase of similar meaning in the passages above.

1  The diamond ring .................................... in the shop window attracted the thief's attention.

2  When the alarm rang, a policeman on .................................... went to investigate.

3  They planned the burglary, using a model of the house, drawn to .................................... .

4  Six men appeared in .................................... yesterday, charged with robbery.

5  We caught most of the gang but one of them .................................... arrest.

6  The police kept .................................... on the house where they planned the robbery.

7  The gang do a good .................................... in stolen goods.

8  The judge is kindly .................................... towards first offenders.

9  After cautioning the girl, the policeman .................................... her go.

10  It's no use making .................................... of theft against someone if you have no evidence.

## Part 2

These two texts are concerned with crimes. For questions **19–22**, choose the answer (**A**, **B**, **C** or **D**) which you think fits best according to the text.

### THE STINGERS STUNG

The police in Britain are copying techniques first developed in the United States to tempt criminals out of hiding. The idea is to transfer the fear of crime from the victims to the criminals themselves. What has proved remarkable so far is the ease with which the villains have fallen into the trap.

In a recent operation based on a film called *Sea of Love*, the police sent letters to 1,000 suspected criminals, telling them they had won a prize of several thousand pounds as part of a government scheme. Within a month no less than 350 had turned up to collect their winnings at the office designated and had been promptly arrested.

Another successful trick was to buy a pub known to be frequented by criminals and man it with police officers. Microphones hidden in the pub recorded the villains' conversations and they were photographed by a camera hidden behind a dart board.

Police officers enjoy taking part in a sting. Apart from its being easier to catch up with suspicious characters in this way, there is fun to be had in having outwitted them.

**19**   Why was the first sting referred to so successful?

**A**   It was derived from a well-known film.

**B**   The criminals were afraid of being treated like victims.

**C**   The criminals were too greedy to resist a free offer.

**D**   The criminals did not realise that the office was a police station.

**20**   What is the main attraction for police officers in taking part in a sting?

**A**   They enjoy acting.

**B**   They can overhear what criminals are saying.

**C**   They can wait for the criminals to come to them, instead of pursuing them.

**D**   It's a pleasure to show criminals you are cleverer than they are.

## MORE WHITE MISCHIEF

The killing of the Earl of Erroll in Kenya, then a British colony, at the height of the Second World War in 1941, remains a mystery officially, though the film relating to it, _White Mischief_, which appeared in 1987, left no doubt as to the identity of the murderer. Erroll was a notorious womaniser who began a passionate affair with the wife of Sir Jock Delves Broughton only two months after her marriage. When he was found shot in his car, it was assumed, as in the film, that the crime was prompted by jealousy, and Broughton was arrested. He was acquitted because the evidence at the trial proved that the bullet used had not come from his revolver. Nevertheless, he committed suicide in England three months later.

The case has been reopened, however, by a new book that claims that Erroll was not such a frivolous character as was previously believed and worked hard for the good of the colony. But he had fascist sympathies and the information he possessed, if passed into German hands, could have endangered the war effort, so he was murdered by the British secret service. The men who provided the author with the evidence are now dead but the account of the killing is hardly convincing. He is supposed to have been shot by a woman he knew very well but did not recognise because she was in disguise. Above all, it seems doubtful that Erroll knew enough to justify execution since the secrets he is said to have possessed were common knowledge.

**21**    What conclusion about the crime was reached in the film _White Mischief_?

    **A**    Erroll was killed by an unknown person.

    **B**    He was killed by a deceived husband.

    **C**    He was killed by a jealous lover.

    **D**    He committed suicide.

**22**    Why does the reviewer of the book reject its arguments?

    **A**    Erroll was a serious man who did not deserve to be killed.

    **B**    The witnesses are no longer alive.

    **C**    Erroll would have recognised the person who killed him.

    **D**    He was not seriously dangerous to the British government.

---

### Active Vocabulary List

These are some words and phrases commonly connected with the subject of crime and the law. If you are not sure of the meaning of any words or phrases, look them up in your dictionary.

| | |
|---|---|
| accuse, arrest, charge, bail | court, evidence, witness, judge, jury |
| lawyer, counsel, prosecute, defend | defendant, plead guilty, not guilty |
| trial, verdict, sentence | break the law, illegal, offence |
| policeman/woman, detective | investigation, suspect, victim |
| crime, steal, rob, burgle, mug | criminal, thief, robber, burglar, mugger |

## Part 3 (Ordering paragraphs)

This article consists of 15 paragraphs. Seven of them have been removed. Choose from the paragraphs **A-H** the one that fits each gap (**23-29**). There is one extra paragraph that does not fit and which you do not need to use.

### NOT SO ELEMENTARY, MY DEAR WATSON

Let's face it, Sherlock Holmes wasn't very good. His methods of detection veered from the merely unscientific to the ludicrous. His famous conclusions about a person's life after a few seconds of observation don't stand up to a moment's scrutiny. Most of the 56 short stories and four novels about him have far-fetched plots and utterly unconvincing characters.

**23**

The next stage in the detective story's development occurred in the 1920s, a sort of golden age dominated by Agatha Christie and three other women writers, Dorothy L Sayers, Ngaio Marsh and Margery Allingham. They set the stereotype for the 'cosy' English whodunnit: a weekend in a country house filled with guests bearing dark secrets, and the lucky presence of an amateur sleuth able to conduct inquiries from the moment the first body is discovered in the library. Never mind the poverty of characterisation. What mattered was whether the vicar could have made that crucial phone call at 2.35 pm and still caught his train connection at 3.05 pm.

**24**

At much the same time, in the United States of the 1930s, a writing revolution had started; it was a natural expression of a raw, vibrant society that had nothing to do with country houses, vicarage tea parties, genteel murderers and polite sleuths. America had one institution that England lacked – the private eye.

**25**

After the Second World War and with these examples in mind, a new generation of readers was no longer prepared to accept the unreality of most English whodunnits. The antidote to the gifted amateur was the professional policeman, as in the 87th Precinct novels of Ed McBain. He wasn't the first to feature realistic police procedure, but his formula created a new genre.

**26**

In Britain, too, the policeman replaced the non-official investigator. Writers would spend time researching policing methods. It became important to get the procedure right. Psychology began to play a bigger part – the whydunnit rather than the whodunnit. The wide-ranging crime novel supplanted the detective story and its narrow boundaries.

**27**

It wasn't until the 1980s that the female hero came into her own. Agatha Christie's Miss Marple did her detective work in the village of St Mary Mead – surely, proportionate to population, the murder capital of the world. But most writers – and women were responsible for at least half of crime fiction – used men as their main investigators. There was a good reason. Until recently, only men occupied senior positions in the police and in the world of the private eye that placed them in the centre of murder inquiries.

**28**

Paretsky uses her PI to point out the ills and corruption of the society around her. Not all the women protagonists of recent crime fiction are quite as combative, but the woman police officer is now firmly established.

**29**

There is evidence that the crime novel has come to the end of its natural life. Murders today are solved with the aid of computers, the Internet and DNA. But pessimistic forecasts over crime fiction's future have been made many times before. Each time, the genre has found a way of reinventing itself. It will do so again.

*Article by Marcel Berlins, © The Times*

**A** In his books, the leading character is, in effect, the squadroom rather than any individual. Crime detection is a joint effort, and, as in real life, there is not always a solution. Some murders don't get solved.

**B** Sara Paretsky wasn't the first to break the mould, but her success started a boom in feminist crime writing in the mid-1980s. Her Chicago private eye, the divorced thirty-something V I Warshawski, lived alone, had occasional affairs, worked out regularly and had a strong social conscience.

**C** Yet more than a century after his creation in 1887, he is still the only fictional detective with an international reputation. The detective story has changed spectacularly in the past 100 years but *The Hound of the Baskervilles* remains a classic. There are many ways of tracing the changes since it was published but the two basic ingredients are the same: someone has been murdered, someone is a murderer and we, the reading public, want to know more.

**D** In the same way, in the 1960s, Chester Himes's Coffin Ed and Grave Digger were unique in being black detectives. The field is now full of every kind of ethnic minority hero.

**E** If precise calculations of time were not the vital clue, puzzles regarding place were set to tease the reader. John Dickson Carr, a writer of prodigious imagination, became the king of the locked-room mystery, where a murder was committed in seemingly impossible circumstances, the body found in a sealed room, for instance, with every exit watched, and no one seen entering or leaving.

**F** A new golden age of crime writing began, with flawed, human coppers at the centre. P D James created the lugubrious Commander Adam Dalgleish in 1962. Ruth Rendell's Chief Inspector Wexford followed, and a whole clutch of other male detectives, the most famous of whom (entirely because of television) was Inspector Morse.

**G** Most of the puzzles in the great detective stories of the past would have been solved long before the book had a chance to develop, some in the first chapter.

**H** This figure has been the basis of American crime fiction since Dashiell Hammett created Sam Spade in *The Maltese Falcon*. The PI was a tough, fast-talking, wise-cracking, whisky drinker who liked his women and his independence. But he had integrity. Raymond Chandler famously described his Los Angeles private eye Philip Marlowe, thus: 'Down these mean streets a man must go who is not himself mean.'

# 7 Reading *House and home*

## Part 1

For questions 1–18, read the texts and decide which answer (**A**, **B**, **C** or **D**) best fits each gap.

### HOUSE PRICES IN LONDON

Before the Second World War, an average family could afford to buy a house in the London area for the equivalent of their annual income; now it would cost four years' salary. Why have prices (1) .............. income to that extent?

There are a number of reasons for the increased demand for housing. Far more marriages (2) .............. , requiring separate accommodation, and children leave home earlier. Apart from that, there has been considerable (3) .............. from other parts of the country. Houses are more expensive nowadays, too, because there are far more 'extras' and local authorities today (4) .............. more stringent controls.

Finally, banks and building societies have a much more (5) .............. attitude nowadays towards granting loans. The combination of increased funds available and a limited supply of housing has sent prices literally soaring through the (6) .............. .

| 1 | **A** | outnumbered | **B** | outstripped | **C** | overreached | **D** | overtaken |
| 2 | **A** | break down | **B** | break out | **C** | fall down | **D** | fall out |
| 3 | **A** | transfer | **B** | removal | **C** | withdrawal | **D** | migration |
| 4 | **A** | compel | **B** | enforce | **C** | exert | **D** | insist |
| 5 | **A** | casual | **B** | careless | **C** | easy-going | **D** | long-suffering |
| 6 | **A** | attic | **B** | roof | **C** | peak | **D** | summit |

### DECORATING THE CHILDREN'S ROOM

There is tremendous (7) .............. on parents these days to decorate a child's room with the child's tastes in mind, something that our own parents would never have taken into (8) .............. . But they may be a far (9) .............. from the parents' taste.

Research indicates that very young children (10) .............. best to details and to movement, but what really stimulates them is their smiling mother's face. (11) .............. the time they are three, they have developed preferences of their own. Pale shades may be tasteful and appeal to adults but bright colours that (12) .............. those of their toys will go down better with the children.

| 7 | **A** | inducement | **B** | incitement | **C** | force | **D** | pressure |
| 8 | **A** | consideration | **B** | mind | **C** | view | **D** | notice |
| 9 | **A** | cry | **B** | distance | **C** | way | **D** | run |
| 10 | **A** | reply | **B** | suit | **C** | respond | **D** | answer |
| 11 | **A** | At | **B** | By | **C** | During | **D** | In |
| 12 | **A** | correspond | **B** | relate | **C** | match | **D** | identify |

## HOUSE FOR SALE – GHOST INCLUDED

Estate agents all agree that a house can get itself a bad (13) ............... . Its past may hang over it like a curse. If buyers learn, for example, that a child fell to its death from the balcony, they will probably (14) .............. of the deal.

While buyers understandably (15) .............. to commit themselves if there is some environmental danger, their reactions to human factors are less predictable. Cases where feelings (16) .............. facts most clearly are in houses where crimes have been committed. The (17) .............. rumour that the house might be haunted by the ghost of the victim will lower the price. But those willing to take a chance may be (18) ............... . Once the crime has been forgotten, they can sell for a big profit.

| 13 | **A** fame | **B** regard | **C** name | **D** celebrity |
|----|----|----|----|----|
| 14 | **A** back out | **B** withdraw | **C** turn back | **D** retire |
| 15 | **A** doubt | **B** delay | **C** hesitate | **D** question |
| 16 | **A** overrate | **B** overcome | **C** outclass | **D** outweigh |
| 17 | **A** mere | **B** only | **C** sheer | **D** sole |
| 18 | **A** benefited | **B** profited | **C** gratified | **D** rewarded |

## Vocabulary Development

Complete the sentences below with a word or phrase taken from the choices for the questions you have answered. The sentences are printed in the same order as the questions. Note the difference between the correct answer below and a phrase of similar meaning in the passages above.

1   It's amazing that couples ................................. over such trivial matters and the marriage ends in divorce.

2   Nowadays the authorities ................................. on the regulations being observed.

3   The authorities ................................. builders to respect the regulations.

4   Far from feeling sorry for him, I can only sympathise with his ................................. wife, who has to put up with his moods.

5   In decorating a room, parents should bear the child's tastes in ................................. .

6   Bright colours ................................. young children best.

7   They like pictures of their favourite TV characters because they can ................................. with them.

8   They decided to ................................. from the deal when they heard what had happened in the house.

9   They're likely to ................................. committing themselves to the purchase until the surveyor has submitted his report.

10   The fact that a famous person has lived there may add to the value of the house, but it wouldn't be wise to ................................. its effect.

## Part 2

These two texts are concerned with the home. For questions **19–22**, choose the answer (**A**, **B**, **C** or **D**) which you think fits best according to the text.

### WHAT SHAPE TABLE?

Most of us only have room in the dining room for one table and shape is normally determined by convenience, but the choice of shape is significant.

Round tables are democratic; no one is given precedence. For that reason politicians describe meetings between representatives of different countries as 'round table conferences', fostering the pleasant illusion that all nations are equal, even though, in George Orwell's famous phrase: 'some are more equal than others.'

In restaurants, however, most tables are either square or oblong. This is partly for reasons of space, but also because they make the waiters' task of serving easier. Above all, bearing in mind the bill and in particular the tip, they enable them to identify the host, preferably seated at the head of an oblong. The Chinese, on the other hand, blending ancient philosophy with common sense, disapprove of sharp edges, and consequently prefer round or oval tables.

Those who manufacture tables to order, catering for people who can afford a number, suggest different ones for different purposes – round tables for friendly gatherings, small oblongs for business meetings, and for banquets with many people invited, long, narrow oblongs, encouraging them to converse with the person opposite.

**19**    What sort of table would you choose if you had to organise an intimate dinner for a Government minister from your country with two assistants, and three visitors of equivalent rank from China?

    **A**   square

    **B**   oval

    **C**   small oblong

    **D**   long oblong

**20**    You are the manager of a restaurant. A firm have booked a table for eight people for their Managing Director, his assistants, an important customer and his adviser. What sort of table will you give them and where will you seat the Managing Director?

    **A**   round, with the Managing Director beside the customer.

    **B**   square, with the Managing Director opposite the customer and his adviser.

    **C**   oblong, with the Managing Director at one end.

    **D**   oblong, with the Managing Director and the customer side by side.

## MAKING A HOUSE PAY FOR ITSELF

The proliferation of fashion magazines featuring the interiors of houses has provided some home owners with an additional source of income. If you don't mind photographers tramping around your house and tripping over the furniture, it's worth their while to take pictures near at hand rather than fly to exotic locations.

A woman who has turned this into a profitable business, currently welcoming photographic crews once or twice a week, says that the secret is to decorate simply and economically and, when changes are necessary, to make them in line with current trends. Crews must have freedom to operate, but she wouldn't allow them in if she wasn't on hand throughout to keep an eye on them. Antiques and family heirlooms should be kept out of harm's way.

The magazine editors, often displaying furniture for advertising purposes, make ease of access their first priority. Lighting is important, the more space available the better, and since shots are often directed at a window, a pleasant view in the background is welcome. It also helps if there are contrasts in surfaces and period features that set off modern developments.

21    The house owner referred to
    **A**    doesn't spend much on the house, knowing photographers make a mess.
    **B**    changes the furniture at regular intervals.
    **C**    stays in the house to prevent things from being stolen.
    **D**    ensures that nothing valuable is damaged.

22    What is the most important feature from the editors' point of view?
    **A**    facility in moving things in and out
    **B**    sufficient lighting to take photographs
    **C**    the view outside
    **D**    the type of decoration

### Active Vocabulary List

These are some words and phrases commonly connected with the subject of house and home. If you are not sure of the meaning of any words or phrases, look them up in your dictionary.

*apartment/flat, block of flats*
*hall of residence*
*bungalow, house*
*detached, semi-detached, terraced house*
*basement, ground floor, first floor*
*landlord/lady, let, rent*
*overlook, view*
*housing estate, suburb, town centre*

*Part 3 (Multiple-choice comprehension)*

Read this article about house-hunting. For questions **23–29**, choose the answer (**A**, **B**, **C** or **D**) which you think fits best according to the text.

### LOVE AT FIRST SIGHT

It is a fact of life that we choose our homes in about three minutes flat, the time it takes to boil an egg. Often the decision is made in the hallway before any other part of the house has even been seen. The choice on which our happiness – or otherwise – will depend is based on nothing more than a sense of atmosphere. A survey shows that as many as 60 per cent of us behave in this way. Practical matters such as the number of bedrooms, the quality of the kitchen, the proximity to shops, transport and schools pale beside this powerful surge of emotion.

Tara Chapman knows well how overwhelming the 'feel good factor' can be. When she first walked into her two-bedroom flat in London she started to cry. 'It was a dark November afternoon. I walked into the living room and burst into tears. It made me feel suddenly at home,' she says. Her work for a television advertising production company in Spain now takes her away for long periods, so she has decided to sell. Her agents are asking nearly £300,000 for the flat and are no doubt hoping that it tugs at someone else's heartstrings. 'I will probably weep when I leave it,' Tara says.

With couples, the 'must have' moment is often accompanied by emotional gestures, as if they are posing for wedding photographs all over again. 'There is a lot of hand holding, then her head goes on his shoulder and you know they want the house. It usually happens in the first room they go into,' says estate agent Melissa Bruce-Jones. 'People are often drawn by the decoration and the possessions of the existing owners. So many houses in London are identical, but if buyers identify with a life style, they want the house.'

The rush of emotion tells an estate agent that a purchase is imminent, but if it comes too soon after the house has been put on the market, it can also cause problems. William Kirkland has just completed the exchange on a house that went on the market ten days ago.

'The buyer went to see it at nine in the morning on the first day,' he says. 'By 10.30 she had made an offer. She just knew the house was right.'

But no other buyer had yet had a chance to see it, and many wanted to. What should he do? 'If she cooled later, then we would lose all the other applicants,' he says. 'They would wonder why the sale had fallen through, and distrust me because I hadn't let them see the house first time round.' And of course other buyers might offer more money, too! The solution was to allow the passionate first buyer

to have the house provided she settled within ten days. She just made it.

Where, then, does this good feeling come from? The 18th-century landscape designer Lancelot 'Capability' Brown knew how to create drama for a big country house; he would arrange it so that the house was approached by a meandering drive that allowed only snatched glimpses of the house before finally revealing the full glory of the façade at the end. This was the kind of experience Charles Illingworth had when he first saw his house in Somerset. 'We were not even looking for a house,' he says. 'We crested the top of the drive and looked down at this amazing view, with the house sitting down below.'

'We didn't need to go into the house. We both knew it was the sort of place we had always wanted to live and bring up children in. We didn't even have children at the time. And the thing was that the pretty side of the house was actually the other side. It was a complete wreck – but it had magic.'

It is not quantifiable criteria that sell houses, but abstract qualities such as charm and potential. Agents agree that the light-socket counters tend not to buy. Nor do those who make multiple visits, who often suffer for their dithering. 'I am told it is like buying a new dress,' says Colin Swait, another agent. 'You go to every shop before you go back to the first one, and sometimes it has been sold.'

What elicits the emotional response that draws the offers is a single stunning room or view. 'Eighteenth-century houses are popular,' says Swait. 'They are the houses of our childhood stories, the houses that appear in literature and costume drama. The houses of our dreams. Any biographer will tell you how important houses are to people, how much we are moved by a sense of place.'

The business of househunting can be something of a nightmare, a bad dream of wrong room sizes and wrong addresses from which we eventually awake with a sense of coming home. Just as long as we know it as such when we get there.

*Article by Caroline McGhee © Telegraph Group Limited*

23    Which of these is decisive for the majority of people buying a house?
     **A**   their first impression
     **B**   the size of the house
     **C**   its condition
     **D**   the area where it is situated

24    What is Tara Chapman saying about her feelings with regard to her flat?
     **A**   They will be the same on leaving as on first sight.
     **B**   She will behave the same way for different reasons.
     **C**   She is sure someone will buy it for the same reasons as she did.
     **D**   She is sad that she will not get a fair price for it.

25    What does Melissa suggest attracts couples to houses?
     **A**   Something that reminds them of their wedding.
     **B**   The fact that a house is different from others they have seen.
     **C**   The contents of the house that the owners are also offering.
     **D**   The feeling that they would like to live like the present owners.

26    Why did Mr Kirkland feel that he had a problem?
     **A**   He was afraid the woman would regret making up her mind so quickly.
     **B**   He thought that her quick decision would put other buyers off.
     **C**   He thought that other buyers would be angry that he hadn't advertised that the house was for sale.
     **D**   He suspected that he could get a better price for the house.

27    What attracted Mr Illingworth and his wife to the house they bought?
     **A**   its situation
     **B**   its general condition
     **C**   its being ideal for their children
     **D**   the fact that they saw its most attractive features first

28    Which buyers are most likely to be disappointed?
     **A**   Those who are unwilling to bargain.
     **B**   Those who worry too much about details.
     **C**   Those who take a long time to make up their minds.
     **D**   Those who rely on first impressions.

29    What sort of warning for buyers is contained in the last sentence?
     **A**   Don't let househunting affect your health!
     **B**   Don't buy anything in an unpleasant area!
     **C**   Don't insist on trying to recreate your childhood home!
     **D**   Make sure that what you buy really suits you!

For questions **1–18**, read the texts and decide which answer (**A**, **B**, **C** or **D**) best fits each gap.

### AN INDIAN WEDDING

When my Indian friend said we were going to a party, the night before a wedding, I (1) ............... that I had not been invited. But he (2) ............... my objections, assuring me that no one (3) ............... if a friend brings a friend along.

In India the marriage is always arranged – love comes later, if at all – and signifies the (4) ............... of two families rather than of the couple, who may not even have met.

The ceremony took place the following evening. It took over two hours but guests were not expected to (5) ............... attention to it all. They wandered in and out and some handed over envelopes full of money which the bride secreted in the (6) ............... of her dress. In the end, the couple got up, took seven steps round the sacred fire, and were formally declared man and wife.

| | | | | | | | | |
|---|---|---|---|---|---|---|---|---|
| **1** | **A** | protested | **B** | opposed | **C** | contradicted | **D** | disagreed |
| **2** | **A** | overturned | **B** | overthrew | **C** | overruled | **D** | overpowered |
| **3** | **A** | annoys | **B** | minds | **C** | resists | **D** | dislikes |
| **4** | **A** | junction | **B** | link | **C** | connection | **D** | union |
| **5** | **A** | give | **B** | pay | **C** | show | **D** | fix |
| **6** | **A** | bends | **B** | curves | **C** | folds | **D** | creases |

### BEING A GRANDFATHER

Grandparents today often write to the newspapers, (7) ............... their inability to make contact with their grandchildren. They are often (8) ............... from them by long distances, as I am from mine, and it takes time for a child to (9) ............... confidence in dealing with an adult.

The first time I was left alone with my two-year-old granddaughter, she looked at me with suspicion. She (10) ............... to go to bed, but a few minutes later I found her sitting on the stairs. I put her to bed again and this time she fell (11) ............... asleep. The next day, my daughter-in-law informed me that I had evidently (12) ............... the test of acceptance. 'He was very gentle,' the little girl had said.

| | | | | | | | | |
|---|---|---|---|---|---|---|---|---|
| **7** | **A** | grieving | **B** | crying | **C** | complaining | **D** | lamenting |
| **8** | **A** | isolated | **B** | detached | **C** | removed | **D** | separated |
| **9** | **A** | obtain | **B** | gain | **C** | win | **D** | grow |
| **10** | **A** | accepted | **B** | conceded | **C** | consented | **D** | submitted |
| **11** | **A** | fast | **B** | well | **C** | quite | **D** | fully |
| **12** | **A** | approved | **B** | carried | **C** | overcome | **D** | passed |

### THE DEVIL YOU KNOW

Whenever the gossip columns feature the (13) ............... of some famous couple's marriage, they are likely to add that the one who has been (14) .............. is seeking consolation in a former relationship. According to marriage (15) ............... experts, women are more likely than men to take this way out of a broken heart situation, but it makes good (16) ............... . Your friends may begin to yawn as you (17) .............. out your tales of woe but your ex may be curious to know what went wrong this time. The relationship may not last, but if you long for security, it may be wise to put your (18) ............... in the devil you know.

| | | | | | | | |
|----|---|--------------|---|--------------|---|--------------|---|
| **13** | **A** | break-off | **B** | break-up | **C** | cut-off | **D** | cut-up |
| **14** | **A** | disgusted | **B** | discharged | **C** | discarded | **D** | disengaged |
| **15** | **A** | assistance | **B** | direction | **C** | guidance | **D** | management |
| **16** | **A** | judgement | **B** | logic | **C** | understanding | **D** | sense |
| **17** | **A** | give | **B** | pour | **C** | send | **D** | throw |
| **18** | **A** | confidence | **B** | hope | **C** | belief | **D** | trust |

## Vocabulary Development

Complete the sentences below with a word or phrase taken from the choices for the questions you have answered. The sentences are printed in the same order as the questions. Note the difference between the correct answer below and a phrase of similar meaning in the passages above.

1 My friend ................................... me, saying that we both had an invitation.

2 They were driving too fast and their car ................................... .

3 The guests did not ................................... much interest in the ceremony.

4 She wrote to her daughter, ................................... of her son's behaviour towards her.

5 I said she looked tired and ought to go to bed and she ................................... my suggestion.

6 It was a great comfort to know that my granddaughter ................................... of me.

7 She's much better now and has been ................................... from hospital.

8 Attending a ................................... course may help you to run your factory, but you can't treat your wife like one of your employees!

9 When she heard that he had been seeing another woman, she decided to ................................... out a challenge to him: Make up your mind – either her or me!

10 She said she always took her troubles to her ex-husband because she had the utmost ................................... in his judgement.

*Part 2*

These two texts are concerned with relationships. For questions **19–22**, choose the answer (**A**, **B**, **C** or **D**) which you think fits best according to the text.

### ONE AND ONLY

The birth rate in most European countries has fallen fast in recent years so the only child is a far more frequent phenomenon. Those who grew up with brothers and sisters used to envy this privileged specimen. This child always comes first, will always be listened to, will never be in doubt that it is loved best, will never be forced to inherit its elders' clothes, will never have its toys stolen or broken. What bliss to be an only child!

Only children of that generation replied that loneliness is far worse, and after being cherished from birth the demands of school life came as a rude shock. Now that many more mothers go out to work, the problem is more acute. Only children are far more often placed in care at an early age, but without the support or even rivalry of siblings at home, they find it more difficult to share or take turns. Teachers report that they are much more likely to be disruptive and argumentative.

**19**     Which heading would be most suitable for the first paragraph?

    **A**    Worrying fall in the birth rate

    **B**    Parents settle for single-child families

    **C**    The spoilt only child

    **D**    The fortunate only child

**20**     In what way are only children worse off today?

    **A**    in their relationships at home

    **B**    in their relationships with other children

    **C**    in their relationships at school

    **D**    in all respects

## THE TROUBLED TEENAGE YEARS

Being a teenager is tough. Tough for the boy or girl, and tough for their parents. All sorts of worries that never before existed come to light at this time, and without the benefit of the hindsight that parents possess, having lived through it, they may seem insurmountable. The most common worries are: *Will I find the right boyfriend or girlfriend?*, *What am doing with my life?* and, last but not least, *My parents don't*

*understand me*. Coupled to these are the stresses created by the pressures of examinations, where once again parents' expectations may be a contributory factor.

Parents notice the signs of stress and often feel guilty, believing that the lack of communication on the teenager's part is their fault. There is a great deal of well-meaning advice on the subject, encouraging teenagers to speak out and parents to listen, but the heart of the problem lies in trust, which should have developed earlier in childhood. Teenagers will find it easier to share their thoughts if they sense that their parents went through similar experiences; parents need to recall what being a teenager was like, and how they got through it.

**21**   What reason is given for teenagers feeling they cannot solve their problems?

   **A**   their lack of experience

   **B**   their relationships with their peer group

   **C**   their relationship with their parents

   **D**   their difficult situation at school

**22**   What is the writer arguing in the second paragraph?

   **A**   Parents are wrong to blame themselves.

   **B**   They should seek professional guidance.

   **C**   They can help if a good relationship already exists.

   **D**   They should put themselves in the teenagers' shoes.

---

**Active Vocabulary List**

These are some words and phrases commonly connected with the subject of relationships. If you are not sure of the meaning of any words or phrases, look them up in your dictionary.

| | |
|---|---|
| *nuclear, extended, one-parent family* | *parents, relations/relatives* |
| *in-laws, stepfather/mother* | *ancestor, descendant* |
| *friendly, sociable, hospitable* | *get on with, be on good terms with* |
| *quarrel, fall out, split up* | *get/be engaged, married, divorced* |

## Part 3 (Ordering paragraphs)

This article consists of 15 paragraphs. Seven of them have been removed. Choose from the paragraphs **A-H** the one that fits each gap (**23-29**). There is one extra paragraph that does not fit and which you do not need to use.

### BORN TO BE TOGETHER

'It was just so unfair. Being criticised for being the same when we shared the same genetic make-up and the same upbringing.' You can still hear the bitterness in the voice of Amrit Kaur Singh, an artist, many years after she was ridiculed at university for producing work that was virtually indistinguishable from that of her identical twin, Rabindra.

**23**

Nowadays, at the age of 35, the Singh twins make a point of it. They dress alike, often work together on the same paintings, and collect joint awards for their internationally acclaimed work. They are inseparable, living together in an extended family near Liverpool, professional twins *par excellence*. Their art creates a delightful world that straddles two cultures.

**24**

This is the challenge facing every twin and every parent of twins: how to find a natural identity and independence in a society that is both fascinated and repelled by the idea of replica human beings. Should individuals with a common gene pool be steered along divergent paths, or should they be encouraged to accept, even celebrate, their sameness?

**25**

Liz has fought to treat her boys as individuals, fighting off attempts by others to lump them together as 'the twins.' They dress differently and sleep in different rooms. On their birthday, they will have two cakes and separate parties with different guests. When young, they attended a playgroup on separate days. At school, Liz requested different classes.

**26**

Her philosophy is not shared by Gina Prince. Her six-year-old twins, Amy and Karina, have spent their childhood in matching outfits. They ride around on identical bikes. Presents must always be the same. They sleep in bunks, one on top of the other. When their school decided to separate them, they were unhappy and so was their mother.

**27**

But treating the girls alike has brought problems as well as benefits. 'I do enjoy the attention when I take them out dressed the same. I also prevent jealousy by always being fair. However, I worry that they won't grow up to lead their own lives. I want them to be more independent but often they still want to be the same. It's very difficult. They are twins, after all. Who am I to force them apart?'

**28**

But according to Gina Siddons, mother of 16-year-old twins and manager of the Twins and Multiple Birth Association, problems often crop up when parents treat twins as a unit. 'The answer is to separate them early,' she says. 'Send them to playgroup on different days, put them in different classes at school. If you dress them the same, it gives other people the message that they are a unit. And there is nothing more disappointing for a child than opening exactly the same presents as his or her twin.'

**29**

It is difficult, however, to feel sad about the Singh twins. The world of their paintings is bright, humorous, intelligent and warm. They are successful. They seem happy. They are doing what they want to do. If the fact that they are doing it together is a problem, then it is our problem, and not theirs.

*Article by Jane Bond © Telegraph Group Limited*

**A** 'People are not sure how to deal with twins. There is a weirdness about the idea that makes people treat them as freaks,' says Liz Traynor, mother of identical seven-year-old twins, John and Angus. 'I didn't want any of that for my two. I wanted them to be like any other child.'

**B** 'You must treat your twins as individuals and make special time for each twin separately. Be relaxed about their shared interests, but don't let them gang up on you. If you have problems, join a twin club for information and support,' she says. 'But what I really cannot approve of is giving joint birthday cakes or presents.'

**C** 'They were quite upset. They are very close. I wanted them to have their own beds but they always end up in the same one. My mother bought them different coats but Amy just wanted Karina's. I buy them the same all the time, just to save arguments,' she says.

**D** The twins themselves appear frequently in their work, always dressed the same, often in mirrored poses, occasionally with one twin standing apart to emphasise her detachment. The same but different, together but apart. It is a fascinating theme, one that has brought them professional recognition and an annoying, but commercially useful, media obsession with their twin status. It is, as they both admit, 'a double-edged sword.'

**E** As for Amrit and Rabindra, she says: 'It is very common for twins to follow the same career path, even when they are comfortable with their own individuality. The Singh twins' experience just shows how we have failed to educate the public on the subject of twins. People think they are copying each other when they are just the same by nature. They end up being forced to make a statement about it. It's sad.'

**F** 'I admit I was paranoid about it when they were little,' she confesses. 'They are extremely alike, even losing teeth at the same times, and many people can't tell them apart, but because of our efforts they have emerged as individuals, with different personalities, different interests and different friends.'

**G** They exchange glances, two tiny, beautiful mirror images, dressed in traditional Sikh costumes that are duplicated down to the last elaborate detail. They both remember the sneering words of the examiners: 'Haven't you ever tried to be different?' 'As if' Amrit says contemptuously, 'we had ever actually tried to be the same.'

**H** Barney Allcock, father of two-year-old twins Alec and Max, agrees with her. 'You've got to treat twins exactly the same; otherwise they fight. They are very rarely split up, they get on well, so what's the point? The more obstacles you put in their way, the more they will break them down. They were born together, and you can't take that closeness away from them.'

## Part I

For questions 1–18, read the texts and decide which answer (**A**, **B**, **C** or **D**) best fits each gap.

### THE MONSTER TOURIST ATTRACTION

Now that (1) ............... -life monsters like the Ceaucescus, who (2) ............... tourists off visiting Romania at all, have disappeared from the scene the tourist trade is making the (3) ............... of its internationally recognised fictitious monster, Count Dracula the vampire. At the Hotel Castel Dracula, the walls are decorated with horrific scenes, while he lies in his coffin, with blood (4) ............... from his pointed teeth. But the atmosphere is genuine enough in the forest outside; there are real wolves (5) ............... among the trees.

Bram Stoker's classic tale was based on Prince Vlad, who was certainly bloodthirsty. The only blood (6) ............... done at his modern castle is done by mosquitoes, but a bright red drink called Dracula's Kiss is served to guests. This is, in fact, made from plums.

| | | | | | | | | |
|---|---|---|---|---|---|---|---|---|
| 1 | **A** | real | **B** | actual | **C** | true | **D** | modern |
| 2 | **A** | turned | **B** | sent | **C** | put | **D** | set |
| 3 | **A** | best | **B** | most | **C** | use | **D** | play |
| 4 | **A** | dripping | **B** | squirting | **C** | drooping | **D** | spilling |
| 5 | **A** | barking | **B** | grunting | **C** | howling | **D** | roaring |
| 6 | **A** | drinking | **B** | sucking | **C** | sipping | **D** | soaking |

### BESIDE THE SEASIDE

At one time, the British spent their annual holiday at a local resort on the coast, (7) ............... pretending that they were enjoying themselves. There was even a song that (8) ............... : 'Oh, I do like to be beside the seaside.' The sea, grey and dirty, discouraged bathing. Parents (9) ............... grimly to deckchairs in the bitterly cold wind, watching their children build sandcastles that blew (10) ............... as soon as erected.

The theory was that, if you were at the seaside, you must be having a good time, though anyone in his right (11) ............... would have gone straight home. It held (12) ............... until cheap flights became available to places where the sun shone and the sea was blue. And then it really became a pleasure to be beside the seaside.

| | | | | | | | | |
|---|---|---|---|---|---|---|---|---|
| 7 | **A** | stiffly | **B** | inflexibly | **C** | hardly | **D** | stubbornly |
| 8 | **A** | reported | **B** | celebrated | **C** | proclaimed | **D** | announced |
| 9 | **A** | clung | **B** | hung | **C** | held | **D** | stuck |
| 10 | **A** | away | **B** | out | **C** | off | **D** | up |
| 11 | **A** | sense | **B** | opinion | **C** | mind | **D** | judgement |
| 12 | **A** | influence | **B** | domination | **C** | sway | **D** | weight |

**VETERAN SAILOR'S CROSSING OF THE ATLANTIC**

A determined woman of 89 accomplished a voyage this summer that she had been planning for most of her life and settled a score with her father, who had (13) .............. her to do it long ago. Helen Tew, (14) .............. as crew by her eldest son, Donald, sailed across the Atlantic and back.

In 1934, her father, Commander Graham, a naval officer, promised they would cross the Atlantic together but left her (15) .............. . When he published an account of his solo voyage, his daughter was still so angry that she (16) .............. to read it. Helen married a naval architect and they hoped to make the crossing in a boat they built but the Second World War (17) .............. out and afterwards they were too busy (18) .............. a family. Now at last she has fulfilled her dream.

| | | | | | | | |
|---|---|---|---|---|---|---|---|
| 13 | A | forbidden | B | prohibited | C | stopped | D | prevented |
| 14 | A | accompanied | B | attended | C | escorted | D | joined |
| 15 | A | back | B | alone | C | behind | D | standing |
| 16 | A | denied | B | refused | C | rejected | D | resisted |
| 17 | A | started | B | set | C | broke | D | burst |
| 18 | A | training | B | nursing | C | raising | D | educating |

## Vocabulary Development

Complete the sentences below with a word or phrase taken from the choices for the questions you have answered. The sentences are printed in the same order as the questions. Note the difference between the correct answer below and a phrase of similar meaning in the passages above.

1   I .................................... off the gas and electricity before going on holiday.

2   The weather here has been awful, but we're making the .................................... of it.

3   We stayed in a farmhouse and could hear the pigs .................................... all night.

4   We .................................... her birthday with dinner at a good restaurant.

5   We .................................... tight to our hats to prevent them from blowing off.

6   She blew .................................... the candles on the cake at her birthday party.

7   His opinion carries some .................................... with the town council.

8   Her father .................................... her from fulfilling her ambition.

9   He set off at such a speed that it left his rivals .................................... .

10  She .................................... that she was still angry with her father.

**Part 2**

These two texts are concerned with different aspects of travel. For questions **19–22**, choose the answer (**A**, **B**, **C** or **D**) which you think fits best according to the text.

## ❖ ——— TRAVEL BOOKS OF THE YEAR ——— ❖

### THE ACCURSED MOUNTAINS
*Robert Carver*

Carver asked the famous travel writer Patrick Leigh-Fermor where he would go if he were young again. The answer was 'Albania, if I could get there'. Carver's remarkable journey was undertaken by all kinds of transport. As the first Briton to visit the country for over 40 years, he was regarded with a mixture of suspicion and bewilderment. One villager refused to believe that in Britain people drove cars instead of riding on donkeys.

### ALMOST HEAVEN
*Martin Fletcher*

Most Americans live in cities but Fletcher, a former correspondent in Washington, set out in an old car to discover the other 25% from the backwoods. There is a mass of useful information here but Fletcher finds room for a whole host of fascinating characters, the patriots, the kind-hearted and the racists. Among them are those dedicated to making Texas independent and those still convinced that the world was created in seven days.

### TRAVELS IN THE WHITE MAN'S GRAVE
*Donald Macintosh*

Macintosh spent thirty years working in West Africa as a tree surveyor. Unlike the many who came and soon died, he was a born survivor, well suited to the region, strong, knowledgeable in his subject, and with a sense of humour. Some might regard his approach to his characters as 'politically incorrect' but this is redeemed by an affectionate, sympathetic portrayal of a dying way of life.

### THE SPIRIT WRESTLERS
*Philip Marsden*

Marsden was in Moscow when he ran into a mysterious character who belonged to a breakaway sect of the Russian Church. His quest for these forgotten people took him to the Turkish border and back through centuries to the original schism. He makes light of the gruelling journey and concentrates on the people. One man says: 'These days I find it difficult to know what's holy'. This could apply to them all.

**19** Which feature is suggested as the most interesting in these books?

    **A**  the problems the writer encountered

    **B**  the strange opinions of the inhabitants

    **C**  the information provided about the country

    **D**  the kind of people the writer met

**20** Which of the four books is as much an autobiography as a travelogue?

    **A**  *The Accursed Mountains*

    **B**  *Almost Heaven*

    **C**  *Travels in the White Man's Grave*

    **D**  *The Spirit Wrestlers*

## HAVE DOG. WILL TRAVEL

Until a year or so ago, the opposite was true in Britain. The law was strictly enforced, so that any domestic animal taken abroad had to spend six months in quarantine on its return, and as a result owners were unwilling to subject their beloved pets to this term of imprisonment and some stayed at home themselves in protest.

In 1994, a devoted dog owner, Lady Fretwell, founded *Passports for Pets* in an attempt to promote a relaxation of the law and new regulations are now in force. Pets must be fitted with an identification chip, be vaccinated against rabies and blood tested six months later, after which their 'passport' will be issued. When crossing the English Channel pets must remain in the car or, if the traveller is on foot, in their own kennel on the deck. On the return journey, they must visit a vet two days before the journey to be treated for ticks and tapeworm, and given a certificate. Otherwise, the statutory six months 'in gaol' will still apply.

Owners are nevertheless warned of the risks from the animal's point of view. On no account should an animal travel if in poor health or if it cannot stand being in a car for long periods. Owners, especially the vast majority who head south for the sunshine, should also bear in mind that lying on the beach and visiting historic monuments are not a dog's idea of a good time. On the whole most dogs would be happier staying at home.

### Active Vocabulary List

These are some words and phrases commonly connected with the subject of travel. If you are not sure of the meaning of any words or phrases, look them up in your dictionary.

*hotel, bed-and-breakfast, camp site*
*tourist resort, culture, night life*
*drive, fly, sail, by land/air/sea*
*airport, arrival, departure, check-in*
*passport control, customs*
*timetable, ticket office, platform*
*agency, brochure, book, reservation*
*sightseeing, excursion*
*by car/train/plane/boat/ferry*
*gate, boarding card*
*port, harbour, board, cabin*
*packing, luggage, trolley*

**21** What is the effect of the changes in the law?

A Pets can now be taken abroad.

B New tests have been imposed on pets taken abroad.

C Owners can now take their pets with them on holiday.

D Now, pets need not be separated from their owners when they come back.

**22** Why are dogs less likely to be pleased by the change than their owners?

A They may fall ill abroad.

B They don't have the same interests as their owners.

C They will be locked inside the car for much of the time.

D They will still be subjected to tests.

## Part 3 (Multiple-choice comprehension)

Read this article about the monument to four United States presidents on Mount Rushmore, South Dakota. For questions **23–29**, choose the answer (**A**, **B**, **C** or **D**) which you think fits best according to the text.

### SHRINE OF AMERICA'S LEADERS

After hours of waiting, the crowd is suddenly hushed, flexed in a silent countdown. The orchestra strikes up the opening chords, the initial volleys thunder from the mountain, the first vast sprays of red and yellow burst into the night sky, trailing swathes of crimson clouds. And as the music settles into its patriotic medley and the falling stars explode into myriad more stars, the clouds part to reveal one of the most familiar – and alien – vistas in the world, the faces of four American presidents, hewn out of the granite cliff and now aglow in the darkness of the summer night. Seventeen minutes later, the fireworks at an end and the floodlighting switched on, the presidents gaze out, earnest and heroic across the rolling plains, and some 25,000 happy Americans make for their cars and buses.

Dutifully dressed in the light-coloured clothing recommended by the National Park Service, they are a picture of America as many still see it, family-oriented, classless and uncynically patriotic. They have had, in many ways, a perfect eve-of-Independence Day* at the country's foremost shrine, the Mount Rushmore National Memorial.

Yet the same all-American self-congratulatory uniformity and contentment that prevailed at Mount Rushmore this holiday week has an exclusive and somewhat dated side to it that raises questions over how successfully the United States is adapting to a more international world. Common language or not, there are times when an English-speaking foreigner – even at the end of a four-year posting – can feel very foreign in America. Thanksgiving Day almost anywhere in the country is one, Independence Day is another, and not primarily because it signifies independence from us. At Mount Rushmore, in the lee of Presidents Washington, Jefferson, Lincoln and Theodore Roosevelt, that foreignness and an attendant unease is multiplied many times over.

Immortalising national leaders at many times their natural size, even posthumously, is a risky business, demonstrated by the many Lenins and Stalins now lying face down and in pieces in the former Soviet Union. And hints of unease can be glimpsed through the troubled history of Mount Rushmore, approved against strong opposition in the economic heyday of the Twenties, begun during the Depression, inaugurated in the year America entered the Second World War, and finally conquering its critics only when it became 'a shrine to American democracy.' Nor has the composition

of the line-up been uncontested. While the merits of Washington, Jefferson and Lincoln, as 'fathers' respectively of independence, the constitution and national reconciliation are rarely questioned, Theodore Roosevelt's place in the cliff has been less secure. Augmenting Mount Rushmore, and if so, by whom, is a perpetual parlour game that has Ronald Reagan in pole position, and even an organised lobby behind him whose voice will surely grow louder after the arch-Cold Warrior's death.

Of more enduring concern perhaps even than the concept and composition of Mount Rushmore is the make-up of the crowds who flock to celebrate their patriotism there. Although almost every state is represented in the licence plates in the vast car parks, the visitors are predominantly white and blue-collar, with scarcely a black, brown or oriental face to be seen. A shrine Mount Rushmore may be, but it is a shrine to a shrinking part of an ever more diverse population that is starting to look to shrines of its own.

A bare half-hour's drive from Mount Rushmore, the Sioux Indian tribe and the family of a second-generation émigré Polish sculptor, Korczak Ziolkowski, are collaborating on another immense rock carving. This one is to Crazy Horse, the Indian warrior leader who, as the story goes, never surrendered or dealt with the white man and was bayoneted to death by an American soldier in September 1877, while observing a truce. The hero's giant head is now complete, and blasting is in progress before work begins on carving the tossing head of his horse. Crazy Horse – begun in 1949 – will not be complete for years, even decades. And while many people combine visits to both monuments, the crowds are more multifarious across race and class, less established and decidedly less complacent.

The two groups, the National Park Service at Mount Rushmore and the determinedly private-sector effort at Crazy Horse, refer to each other in their literature and speak warily of complementing each other. But Crazy Horse, if and when complete, will be bigger and more aggressive than the presidents, who seem at first sight and in daylight to be smaller and less dominant than all the many pictures suggest. Given all the disparities, it is hard to believe their respective adherents will find sharing the territory any easier than their real-life heroes before them.

---

* July 3rd

*Article by Mary Dejevsky © Independent Newspapers (UK) Ltd*

23  What is the writer describing in the first paragraph?
    **A**  the inauguration of a national monument
    **B**  the beginning of an annual celebration
    **C**  the climax of an annual celebration
    **D**  a reunion in honour of some past presidents of the United States

24  What does the writer tell us about herself in the third paragraph?
    **A**  She speaks English although it is not her native language.
    **B**  She is a British journalist sent by her newspaper to report this event.
    **C**  She resents the fact that Americans celebrate independence from Britain.
    **D**  She finds celebrations of this kind disquieting and rather old-fashioned.

25  What is the main risk involved in building such monuments?
    **A**  People may object to the expense when the national economy is in crisis.
    **B**  There may be controversy over which presidents should be commemorated.
    **C**  Pressure groups may insist on honouring unpopular presidents.
    **D**  Present leaders may not be favourably regarded in the future.

26  What sort of people form the majority of the crowd at Mount Rushmore?
    **A**  representatives of all the United States
    **B**  people of all races and complexions
    **C**  middle-class white people
    **D**  working-class white people

27  Why does it appear that the Sioux people chose to honour Crazy Horse?
    **A**  He was their paramount chief.
    **B**  He never gave in to the whites.
    **C**  He was treacherously killed.
    **D**  He came from that part of the country.

28  What difference between the crowds visiting the two monuments does the writer emphasise?
    The Crazy Horse group
    **A**  are not nearly so contented with the way things are.
    **B**  are more working class.
    **C**  only visit the monument to their own people.
    **D**  are much more insecure because of their varied background.

29  What is her view of the relationship between the people who look after the two monuments?
    **A**  on very good terms, praising one another
    **B**  respectful but not altogether trusting
    **C**  fierce rivalry between public service and private enterprise
    **D**  the Mount Rushmore group are afraid that the Crazy Horse group will eventually
        dominate them

## Part 1

For questions 1–18, read the texts and decide which answer (**A, B, C** or **D**) best fits each gap.

### TRAVEL WITHOUT TEARS

Asked for their private definition of hell, many parents would think of a long car journey with young children. One I know remembers singing at the (1) .............. of her voice to (2) .............. the persistent noise of the baby crying and pulling up at the roadside and (3) .............. to go any further to stop the older ones fighting.

The answer is to keep the younger children amused by letting them take their favourite games. Older ones can benefit from getting (4) .............. in the journey, playing games requiring observation. See who can (5) .............. the pub name with the most legs – the Red Lion scores four, the Bell nothing, and the winner is the one who first (6) .............. eyes on the Coach and Horses.

| | | | | | | | | | |
|---|---|---|---|---|---|---|---|---|---|
| 1 | **A** | height | **B** | peak | **C** | summit | **D** | top |
| 2 | **A** | bury | **B** | drown | **C** | sink | **D** | destroy |
| 3 | **A** | denying | **B** | rejecting | **C** | refusing | **D** | resisting |
| 4 | **A** | involved | **B** | mixed | **C** | related | **D** | implied |
| 5 | **A** | detect | **B** | view | **C** | glance | **D** | spot |
| 6 | **A** | sets | **B** | puts | **C** | gets | **D** | makes |

### WAINEWRIGHT THE POISONER

This is the title of a new biography, though there is no proof that the man in (7) .............. ever poisoned anyone. Wainewright, born in 1794, was brought up by his grandfather, a miser. At his death, Wainewright committed his only demonstrable crime, forging signatures to obtain his entire (8) .............. .

But an uncle who had been left the (9) .............. of the grandfather's estate died while Wainewright was staying with him, followed by Wainewright's mother-in-law. Wainewright then persuaded his sister-in-law to (10) .............. her life heavily and she died soon after making her will. He was not put on trial until 12 years later, when his forgery came to (11) .............. . He was sent to a penal colony, where he died, never (12) .............. of poisoning except in the popular mind.

| | | | | | | | | | |
|---|---|---|---|---|---|---|---|---|---|
| 7 | **A** | reference | **B** | question | **C** | examination | **D** | review |
| 8 | **A** | heritage | **B** | heirloom | **C** | dowry | **D** | inheritance |
| 9 | **A** | bulk | **B** | majority | **C** | most | **D** | quantity |
| 10 | **A** | secure | **B** | insure | **C** | pledge | **D** | endorse |
| 11 | **A** | knowledge | **B** | discovery | **C** | exposure | **D** | light |
| 12 | **A** | arrested | **B** | prosecuted | **C** | convicted | **D** | condemned |

### SOME LIKE IT COLD

Most people dread the onset of winter with its usual accompaniment of heavy colds, (13) .............. throats and days off work but do not accept that this may be due to their houses getting artificially warmer. As soon as the central heating is turned on, doctors' waiting rooms (14) .............. with shivering patients. The change in the atmosphere dries out the air and the body responds by releasing chemicals to (15) .............. with it. More blood is pumped into the nose and before long the person is (16) .............. .

There are alternative ways of preparing for cold weather. The most obvious is to wear extra (17) .............. of clothing both indoors and out. But most people (18) .............. that. They would rather have the same temperature all the year round.

| 13 | **A** | raw | **B** | sick | **C** | sore | **D** | tender |
|----|-------|-----|-------|------|-------|------|-------|--------|
| 14 | **A** | crowd | **B** | flock | **C** | outnumber | **D** | overflow |
| 15 | **A** | manage | **B** | compete | **C** | cope | **D** | balance |
| 16 | **A** | sneezing | **B** | smelling | **C** | snorting | **D** | snoring |
| 17 | **A** | covers | **B** | layers | **C** | coats | **D** | tiers |
| 18 | **A** | disregard | **B** | decline | **C** | discard | **D** | reject |

**Tip**

*You have one hour 30 minutes to complete the whole test. Do not spend too long on any one part, and remember that questions 1-18 are worth one mark, questions 19-40 are worth two!*

**Part 2**

You are going to read four texts which are all concerned in some way with travel. For questions **19–26**, choose the answer (**A**, **B**, **C** or **D**) which you think fits best according to the text.

---

#### THE SMALL CAR THAT TYPIFIED BRITAIN

The car that one saw everywhere in the 1960s and which seemed to represent the cheeky, cheerful spirit of a younger generation not old enough to remember the War was the Mini. When tiny German bubble cars became popular, the British Motor Corporation demanded a rival model that would leave the foreigners standing. The Mini was born and in 1964 a souped-up version called the Mini-Cooper won the Monte Carlo rally. All the trend setters among the young, from Princess Margaret to the Beatles, rushed to buy one, and for a few years this brisk little car was identified with everything 'best and British'.

What was overlooked in all the excitement and flag waving was that the designer, Alec Issigonis, was a Greek, with a German mother, who had been brought to England when young and had a splendid disregard for such hallowed conventions as market research – 'bunk' – and team work – 'a camel is a horse designed by a committee'.

Over five million Minis were built and sold but they ceased to attract when the 1960s generation got married and had children. The Mini had ample space in front for driver and passenger but there was no room in the boot for any luggage bigger than a handbag.

Now this famous symbol of 'British' ingenuity is being revived, at least in its fast, Mini-Cooper form. It will be manufactured by BMW in Munich!

---

19  What was the secret of the Mini's success, in the writer's opinion?

A   its speed

B   its lively appearance and performance

C   its having been produced by the national industry

D   its appeal to members of society

20  How did the popular conception of the Mini differ from the reality?

A   The designer defied convention.

B   The car had not been produced as a team effort.

C   The designer was only British by adoption.

D   The car did not really have as much room inside as appeared.

### WHICH ISLAND IN THE CARIBBEAN?

*Bonaire*

A sleepy coral island with some of the world's best diving on well-protected reefs. No news, don't bother to put on shoes, and don't ever dress for dinner! It hardly ever rains.

*Jamaica*

Brash and self-assured, with a reputation for violence, not entirely justified. You can go rafting on the rivers, climb the mountains. The food is first-class.

*Grand Cayman*

A five-star cure for stressed American millionaires. The beaches are safe, the food familiar, the supermarkets stacked. The calm sea makes it the ideal place to learn to dive.

*St Kitts*

Once famous for its sugar, but now the mills are deserted in the rich volcanic landscape. Deserted beaches miles from anywhere. Go while it is still unspoilt and they haven't had time to build huge hotels.

*Dominica*

Wonderful rainforest scenery but little visited because it has no famous beaches. But there are fine walks to volcanic wonders if you can stand the pace.

*St Lucia*

The favourite spot for honeymooners, with tropical scenery and romantic views. There are safe beaches on the north coast and friendly night life.

**21**   Which island would appeal most to those who want to get away from it all?

    **A**   Bonaire

    **B**   Grand Cayman

    **C**   Dominica

    **D**   St Kitts

**22**   Which island would be preferred by those who think there's no place like home?

    **A**   Bonaire

    **B**   Grand Cayman

    **C**   Jamaica

    **D**   St Lucia

### A FAVOURITE FOREIGN CITY

My first adult holiday abroad with a friend was to a city I've loved ever since. I'm not sure why we chose it. It had a free-and-easy reputation at a time when the lure of sun, sand and night life, which has caused a younger generation to flock to the Mediterranean islands, was less pronounced. At that time, visiting the islands required a long, uncomfortable journey by train and ferry, and the local regulations were considerably more strait-laced. Indeed, when I first visited Ibiza two years later, I discovered that couples embracing in public were likely to be arrested.

My friend and I went north instead, across the North Sea to Copenhagen. The weather that fortnight was better than expected but my abiding memory is of the people. Their English was astonishingly fluent. One afternoon, a middle-aged man, obviously the worse for drink, lurched towards us in the street and when we clearly failed to understand his question, switched into English without hesitation or slurring a word and said: 'Would you be so kind as to direct me to the nearest bar?'

Above all, unlike most of the English in those days, they were obviously having a good time. Their working day began early and ended at 4pm. It was a wonderful sight to see everyone streaming home on buses or bicycles, eager to tear off their office clothes and dress up for an evening out in the Tivoli Gardens, crowded with happy, laughing people.

23  In what way was Copenhagen more attractive to the writer and his friend than the Mediterranean at that time?
  A  They felt they would be free to enjoy themselves more.
  B  There was not such a great contrast in the weather.
  C  They were afraid of getting into trouble if they went south.
  D  The islands were further away and could only be reached by sea.

24  What impressed the writer most about the people of Copenhagen?
  A  their linguistic ability
  B  their enjoyment of life
  C  their capacity for alcohol
  D  the contrast between them and the people at home

## DISNEYWORLD – PLUS AND MINUS

Some years after developing the animated cartoon and inventing characters like Mickey Mouse, Walt Disney turned his attention to building parks where parents could go on holiday with their children. Now they are among the most popular resorts in the world, but what is responsible for their special appeal? One important factor is that they keep the real world at arms' length. If they search your bag, they do it with a smile. You won't see rubbish trucks clearing up the mess; it's all done at night. They even keep the gardeners cutting the lawns out of sight during the day.

Critics tend to be those who resent being taken care of by people with a perpetual grin on their faces. They grumble that the child who cries because she's dropped her ice cream and is promptly handed another one by a kind attendant may not get the same treatment from her parents if she drops it in the street tomorrow. If she ever visits a wildlife park in Africa, the wardens won't be trailing round behind the animals cleaning up the dirt.

In effect, the key to Disney's success is very much like the formula for the success of its founder's films. Everything has been carefully thought out so it's always under control. If you don't like your every need to have been anticipated and if the unrelenting attempt to keep you happy drives you mad, stay away!

**25** Which is the main attraction of the theme parks referred to in the first paragraph?
 **A** They are unreal.
 **B** They are a means of escape.
 **C** They are very clean.
 **D** The staff are polite and charming.

**26** Why do some people think that they are not good training for children?
 **A** Children should not be so carefully looked after.
 **B** They will expect their parents to spoil them in the same way.
 **C** It is ridiculous to think that animals are not dirty.
 **D** The parks give a false impression of the world.

## Part 3

This article consists of 15 paragraphs. Seven of them have been removed. Choose from the paragraphs **A–H** the one that fits each gap (**27–33**). There is one extra paragraph that does not fit and which you do not need to use.

### WHERE THE WILDLIFE IS

How satisfying to pull a chain again! Something went out of British plumbing with the arrival of the integrated cistern, but everything that went out of British plumbing with the Victorians has been reinstated in the stateliest form in the bathroom of our suite at the Pool House Hotel. If only for that achievement alone, it deserves its AA accolade, awarded last Thursday, of *Scottish Hotel of the Year*.

**27**

In Wester Ross, the old parish of Gairloch, a glorious body of country between the long sea arms of Loch Torridon and Loch Broom, has all the classic components of the West Highland landscape. It has the mighty Torridon range, the oldest rock in Britain, and Loch Maree, an inland loch more beautiful than any other, including Loch Lomond. It also has a lonely coast, sandy bays, leafy glens, and numerous whitewashed villages.

**28**

The Pool House building on the loch's foreshore, for example, where the River Ewe enters the lake after a short but vigorous journey from Loch Maree, doesn't look like a traditional Highland lodge. But scrape away the white paint and you will expose pink Torridon sandstone, the preferred building blocks of local landowners for three centuries.

**29**

Osgood Mackenzie, who caused thin, acid layers of peat on a windswept headland to bloom with the trees, shrubs and flowers of the temperate world from Chile to Tasmania, lived for a time in Pool House while he worked obsessively on his horticultural masterpiece. Meanwhile his English wife whiled away the hours by carving a chain of Tudor roses in the banisters of the central staircase.

**30**

When the present owners, the Harrison family, made the decision to replace their 13 bedrooms with four themed suites it was Liz Miles who became the creative force. Liz tracked down the extravagant wallpapers and most of the antique furniture and fittings.

**31**

With some reluctance, my husband and I desert the sumptuous fantasy of our ship, *Campania,* to confront the reality of the weather. As enthusiasts for the elemental challenge of the West Highland seaboard, we have a busy programme: a rugged walk, a wildlife cruise, and, as the softest option available, a visit to Inverewe Garden.

**32**

The headland couldn't be more exposed, but the squalls of rain beating in from the Atlantic sail over our heads en route to the mountains. We flush grouse and snipe from the heather on our three-hour walk and glimpse red deer. By the time we reach the sea, there are shafts of sunlight striking the wings of the sea birds.

**33**

We don't. But we do see grey seals and a whole range of rare seabirds. Warblers and other songbirds attend our visit to Inverewe Garden, now owned and maintained by the National Trust for Scotland and not perhaps at their best as summer gives way to autumn. But they are still remarkable.

*Article by Julie Davidson © Telegraph Group Limited*

**A** The Mackenzie family was dominant in this part of the country. Pool House's golden age was Victorian, when the Highlands became the sporting playground for the gentry. There were salmon in the River Ewe, deer to stalk and grouse to shoot, but for a time the lodge was home to one of the less predatory Mackenzies, a man who liked to let things grow rather than cut them down.

**B** There was only one willow tree on the promontory where Osgood Mackenzie began his project in 1862. Now there is a prodigious stand of native woodland, planted to supply the windbreak for his exotic trees and shrubs. The contrast is beautiful.

**C** Some visitors say they would be willing to pay merely to tour the rooms. Many are especially fascinated with *Diadem,* which is modelled on the style of a first-class cabin on the liner *Titanic.* All the suites are named after warships as a tribute to Pool House's function during the Second World War, when it was the Navy's headquarters for co-ordinating the North Atlantic convoys.

**D** Not all these cottages are second homes or self-catering units. The scattered 'capital' of the parish, Gairloch, is something of a boom community, with energetic young locals raising new homes on scenic building plots. At nearby Poolewe, which has the botanical curiosity and tourist attraction of Inverewe Gardens, an old shooting lodge is turning back the clock to find a future.

**E** We usually do our own route finding but we want to investigate Rua Reidh Lighthouse, where Fran Cree and Chris Barrett run residential walking and activity holidays on one of the most remote headlands of the mainland. Just getting there is an adventure, and the airy nature of the clifftop paths makes us glad of the expert presence of Chris, who is a member of the local mountain rescue team.

**F** Seldom has washing been such a treat. As I wallow beneath the cascading canopy of the Shanks Independent Spray Bath (built in Glasgow in 1875) I feel a certain kinship with the grey seal idling in the water outside. From the bathroom window I can see the glassy surface of Loch Ewe, and much of its wildlife.

**G** Our tally of wildlife soars on the sturdy *Starquest,* which skipper Ian Birks steers to the wide mouth of Loch Gairloch. It's the whale watching season and it's part of Ian's purpose to monitor their movements for the Sea Watch Foundation. 'But I never advertise these trips as whale-watching cruises, otherwise people expect to see whales.'

**H** The carvings are still there, one of the few remnants of the 19th century to survive. How can this be? From the outside Pool House may look like an inn with 1960s additions; step inside and you enter into the rich, decorative interior of a Victorian country house. Yet almost all its finest features have been retrieved from architectural salvage yards and put in place over the past three years.

## Part 4

You are going to read a review of a recently published biography. For questions **34–40**, choose the answer (**A, B, C** or **D**) which you think fits best according to the text.

---

### A CIRCLE OF SISTERS: ALICE KIPLING, GEORGIANA BURNE-JONES, AGNES POYNTER AND LOUISA BALDWIN
*by Judith Flanders*

The Macdonald sisters were not a particularly promising crew. Pretty, but not beautiful, bright but not educated, as the daughters of a Methodist minister they could hardly be counted as the last word in glamour. Yet the four girls who were born between 1837 and 1845 (the family numbered eight in all) ended up far away from the dusty life of the provincial chapel into which they had been born.

This being mid-Victorian Britain, the Macdonalds' social transformation came about through their relationships with important or interesting men. Alice Macdonald married an art teacher, followed him to India, and gave birth to Rudyard Kipling. Georgiana married the painter Edward Burne-Jones and ended up with a title, although as a lifelong radical, she felt awkward about it.

Agnes married Edward Poynter, who managed to get most of the British art establishment under his control. At one point he was running the Royal Academy and the National Gallery as well as the Tate. And Louisa married the wealthy Midlands industrialist Alfred Baldwin and produced the good, kind boy who would eventually become the Conservative Prime Minister, Stanley Baldwin.

Although their story sounds superficially like a female version of one of those rags-to-riches tales so beloved of early-Victorian moralists, the Macdonald sisters did not live happily ever after. From the moment they left home, they seem to have found their husbands difficult and their children disappointing.

Ned Burne-Jones may have been a fine painter and a charming man, but he led Georgie a horrible dance with his long, anguished love affairs with other women. Their son Phil was a weak, lonely snob, while his sister Margaret was just plain odd. She made her husband turn down the mastership of Balliol College, Oxford because she did not want to move away from her father in Fulham.

The other sisters fared little better. Alice Kipling may have been hugely proud of her son's success as a writer, but she had to cope with a daughter-in-law who saw it as her job to keep 'Ruddy' as far away from his mother as possible. Louisa Baldwin took to her bed for months at a time, perhaps because her husband, though well-behaved, was rather dull. At one stage she was dosing herself with a bottle of champagne a day.

Agnes may have become Lady Poynter, but she had to endure her husband's deep depressions, not to mention her sons' disappointing careers; they were always leaning on assorted Kiplings and Baldwins for the next job.

Judith Flanders is very good at understanding how families work. With an acute eye, she charts the constant shifts of allegiance and distance that marked the Macdonald siblings' relationships with one another. They were not, on the whole, very good at talking to each other. Instead, their most pressing needs and wounding hurts were expressed through small, unspoken acts. In 1866, Alice, for instance, took well over two months before she got round to writing to her sisters to congratulate them on their marriages.

Where Flanders is less good, however, is in her understanding of the historical background to the Macdonalds' story, at times resorting to generalisations about 'Victorian women' that are blunt and old-hat. This is odd because she is interested in the bigger picture, shoe-horning a great deal of extraneous detail into her narrative. She insists on telling us, for example, how much money a household could make from its waste paper, and just how long mourning should last.

Unfortunately, though, Flanders misunderstands the nature of many of her sources, reading prescriptive literature as if it were a description of how people actually lived. Recent work by professional historians has revealed that the slew of housekeeping 'how-to' books which came onto the market in mid-Victorian Britain tell us more about the fantasies and aspirations of the middle classes than about their everyday reality. The effect of taking these sources as gospel is much the same as a writer 100 years from now assuming that a large number of British women in the early 21st century were busy being domestic goddesses.

These difficulties aside, *A Circle of Sisters* is a good debut effort. Flanders shows herself equal to the tricky business of keeping all the threads of her story going, made doubly confusing by the Victorians' habit of giving everyone in a family the same name. What her book lacks in historical understanding it makes up for in its sharp awareness of family dynamics and the realisation that some things, at least, never change.

*Review by Kathryn Hughes,* © Telegraph Group Limited

**34** How did the Macdonald sisters achieve their position in society?

    **A** by their physical attraction

    **B** by their intelligence

    **C** by their family background

    **D** by marriage

**35** How did their lives differ from the typical popular story of the time?

    **A** They were quite well off in childhood.

    **B** They did not behave as well as the typical heroine.

    **C** They did not find attractive men to marry.

    **D** Their story did not have a happy ending.

**36** What impression are we given of Louisa?

    **A** She was bored.

    **B** She was lazy.

    **C** She was upset by her husband's treatment of her.

    **D** She was disappointed by her children.

**37** Which of the following best describes the relationship between the sisters?

    **A** dislike

    **B** resentment

    **C** indifference

    **D** contempt

**38** What does the reviewer regard as the best feature of the book?

    **A** the overall presentation of the historical period

    **B** the wealth of detail

    **C** historical accuracy

    **D** its comprehension of family relationships

**39** What does she regard as its main weakness?

    **A** statements that are not supported by the evidence

    **B** irrelevant information distracting the reader

    **C** acceptance of contemporary accounts as the whole truth

    **D** inability to relate the period to the modern situation

**40** What was the most difficult problem the biographer had to overcome?

    **A** lack of experience in writing biography

    **B** organisation of the different strands of narrative

    **C** confusion between the characters

    **D** showing the differences between society then and now

**Reading** *Neighbourhood*

For questions 1–18, read the texts and decide which answer (**A**, **B**, **C** or **D**) best fits each gap.

### No More Cock-a-Doodle Do

The crowing of cockerels (1) .............. a practical purpose in the days before alarm clocks, waking villagers for their day's work. Now a resident's complaint in a Cumbrian village has led to the owners of 200 birds being told to take steps to ensure that the noise (2) .............. . They must either keep the birds in darkness until later in the day, in this way (3) .............. the dawn chorus to a more convenient time, or (4) .............. them in crates, which will make it impossible for them to (5) .............. back their heads to crow. The council was (6) .............. to act but felt obliged to do so, saying that noise abatement is as much its concern in the country as in towns.

| | | | | | | | |
|---|---|---|---|---|---|---|---|
| **1** | **A** followed | **B** took up | **C** served | **D** carried on |
| **2** | **A** dies down | **B** leaves off | **C** drops out | **D** dries up |
| **3** | **A** delaying | **B** reserving | **C** postponing | **D** adjourning |
| **4** | **A** confine | **B** restrain | **C** detain | **D** restrict |
| **5** | **A** pull | **B** put | **C** bend | **D** throw |
| **6** | **A** indisposed | **B** unprepared | **C** reluctant | **D** regretful |

### End of the Road for the Cul-de-sac

Twenty years ago, planners felt that the cul-de-sac had everything to (7) .............. it. It enabled families to maintain their (8) .............. but at the same time to get to know their nearest neighbours. Cul-de-sacs were linked by footpaths, where children could play safely, and cars only entered to park since there was no exit.

Unfortunately there is another (9) .............. to the coin. There are fewer burglaries in terraced houses, built back to back, because there is no way in (10) .............. through the front door. But where cul-de-sacs are linked by footpaths adjacent to back gardens, houses become easily (11) .............. to burglars and the footpaths provide a means of escape. Finally, these newer housing developments appeal to working couples, so they are mainly (12) .............. during the day.

| | | | | | | | |
|---|---|---|---|---|---|---|---|
| **7** | **A** advise | **B** propose | **C** advocate | **D** recommend |
| **8** | **A** solitude | **B** privacy | **C** retirement | **D** isolation |
| **9** | **A** face | **B** shape | **C** head | **D** side |
| **10** | **A** only | **B** except | **C** unless | **D** just |
| **11** | **A** accessible | **B** approachable | **C** reachable | **D** obtainable |
| **12** | **A** abandoned | **B** absented | **C** unoccupied | **D** uninhabited |

## SILENCE THAT BELL!

In 1999, the Queen visited a small town in Essex to (13) .............. a monument, a glass tower housing eight bells. But the bells have never been (14) .............. , except illegally on the last night of the century.

The tower was the brain child of Canon Webber, at one time chaplain to the Queen. But what she did not know was that Mr Webber and the parish council had never paid the builders' (15) .............. and cheques he signed were (16) .............. , as no funds were available to meet them.

Local opinion is now divided. Some think he should be arrested for (17) .............. , while others argue that he has not profited personally. The parish council no longer have anything to do with him, claiming that he kept them in (18) .............. throughout.

| | | | | | | | |
|---|---|---|---|---|---|---|---|
| 13 | A commence | B inaugurate | C initiate | D launch |
| 14 | A sounded | B clanged | C rung | D played |
| 15 | A bill | B wage | C cost | D expense |
| 16 | A counted out | B thrown out | C sent back | D paid back |
| 17 | A theft | B fraud | C robbery | D debt |
| 18 | A darkness | B mystery | C obscurity | D ignorance |

## Vocabulary Development

Complete the sentences below with a word or phrase taken from the choices for the questions you have answered. The sentences are printed in the same order as the questions. Note the difference between the correct answer below and a phrase of similar meaning in the passages above.

1 The job proved more complicated than I expected and .............................. most of the morning.

2 The player was so angry that his team mates had to .............................. him from hitting the referee.

3 The leading actor is .............................. and will be unable to take part this evening.

4 I've left my key indoors and can't get in .............................. I climb through the window.

5 Property sales have increased since mortgages became more easily .............................. .

6 People once lived on the island but now it is .............................. .

7 In view of the scandal, the Queen would probably have preferred to .............................. a ship.

8 A siren .............................. at the factory in the old days to tell workers it was time to start work.

9 The council were not informed of the .............................. of the work that was done.

10 They said that the canon's behaviour was a .............................. to them.

## Part 2

These two texts are concerned with different neighbourhoods. For questions **19–22**, choose the answer (**A**, **B**, **C** or **D**) which you think fits best according to the text.

## VILLAGE OF THE YEAR

*These six villages were the winners of awards in different regions for their efforts to improve their facilities. Read the comments of the judges.*

### East Keswick

An ancient village that has produced a best-selling historical guide, all the profits being spent on improving youth facilities. The villagers appreciate their inheritance and make the most of it.

### Egerton

The village looks after all species of wildlife and has built a recreation ground. Future plans include a skateboard park for teenagers. The community collected £125,000 to build a new village hall.

### Lubenham

Under threat of being swallowed by a town nearby, villagers aim to preserve their historical past but are modern enough to have a website to deal with local problems. They regret the loss of the post office.

### Llandrinio

The villagers run a 50/50 shop, paying half the profit to the community. This has brought hope to a place that has lost its school, and suffered serious flooding and an outbreak of foot-and-mouth disease among the cattle.

### Holywell

Villagers have transformed a quarry into a bird sanctuary, set up a café for 13-18 year olds, and have just opened a large sports complex. They are determined to prevent a road being built that would cut through the village.

### Congresbury

Congresbury is divided east to west by a busy road, and north to south by a river. Villagers have built a bridge to link the two halves. They have opened a café where young people can meet.

19    Where would you choose to live if you had two teenage children?

    **A**   East Keswick

    **B**   Holywell

    **C**   Egerton

    **D**   Congresbury

20    Which village has had the greatest problems to deal with?

    **A**   Lubenham

    **B**   Holywell

    **C**   Llandrinio

    **D**   Congresbury

## AN OLD YORKSHIRE TOWN

A town's past is often clearly commemorated in its street names. Wednesday Market and Saturday Market are two street names in Beverley, along with North Bar Within and North Bar Without. Beverley is a town with a rich mercantile and clerical past, evident in its 13th century Gothic church and its Guildhall, a mediaeval building recently restored.

In this rapidly growing town in the East Riding of Yorkshire, cattle are no longer sold in the market, which is now held only on Saturdays. The largest local employer is a chemical firm, and another of its major employers is the area council.

The town is only 10 miles from the city of Hull but its property market is far from depressed. A house that struggles to sell for £15,000 in Hull will fetch at least treble that amount in Beverley. A local estate agent says the property market here is as buoyant as it has been for a long time. The town is especially attractive to people commuting to the city and outsiders coming from the more expensive areas of the country further south who find work in the neighbourhood.

21　Which of the streets mentioned in the first paragraph no longer lives up to its name?

   **A**　Wednesday Market

   **B**　Saturday Market

   **C**　North Bar Within

   **D**　North Bar Without

22　What reason is given for the rapid growth in the population of the town?

   **A**　There is a chemical factory there.

   **B**　Property is cheap.

   **C**　The town has a rich history.

   **D**　It is convenient for those working in Hull and not too dear.

### Active Vocabulary List

These are some words and phrases commonly connected with the subject of the neighbourhood. If you are not sure of the meaning of any words or phrases, look them up in your dictionary.

| | |
|---|---|
| *public services* | *education, health* |
| *arts, sports facilities* | *commemoration* |
| *transport, traffic, parking* | *ring road, by-pass* |
| *supermarket, mall, corner shop* | *town/city centre, suburbs, outskirts* |

## Part 3 (Multiple-choice comprehension)

Read this account of an unusual holiday resort on the south coast of England. For questions **23–29**, choose the answer (**A**, **B**, **C** or **D**) which you think fits best according to the text.

### LIFE'S A BEACH HUT

The holiday huts that are dug into the side of Treninnow Cliff have flushing outside toilets (if they're lucky) but no mains electricity, yet they are still heaven to their owners. Pip Bond searches in his wallet for a photograph of himself as a boy standing just where he is now. 'This hut has been in my family for three generations,' he says, 'and that's a typical history.'

Between the wars the tenant farmers let local families pitch bell tents at first and then tea-huts for nominal rents. It was before planning regulations, so the huts sprang up in a fashion that was at once anarchic and strictly governed by the landscape.

The Wilmots' present, comparatively grand 'chalet' started out as one garden shed, then a sibling plonked down another a few feet away, then one of the children from the next generation put up a couple of plywood walls to link the two. The flimsiness of the hut itself and its proportions are in striking contrast to the solidity of the 1930s dresser, which sits like an armoured tank in a doll's house. 'The huts have been built round the furniture,' says Ian, a third-generation Treninnow Wilmot. Certainly his hut's window, with its spectacular sea view, looks as if it has been propped up on the end of a worn 1970s sofa.

Most of the huts have gas lights but no heating. In the spring, the inside walls are covered by explosions of mould yet the tenants have been battling to keep the Treninnow community exactly as it is. In 1973 Treninnow Cliff passed from the Mount Edgcumbe Estate to, jointly, Plymouth City Council and Cornwall County Council. 'Cornwall's policy was to clear the cliffs of chalets completely. They finally settled for rent increases that amount to 65 per cent. We've fought hard and got reasonable terms,' says Pip Bond, secretary of the Tenants' Association. Since the lease costs were only nominal in the first place, the total rise of a few hundred pounds a year might not seem massive. But it could easily be enough to change the character of the community completely. 'About 25 to 30 per cent of the hut owners are pensioners, and the worry is that they'll be priced out,' says Pip.

The fact that most families have been coming to the Treninnow huts for generations is crucial to the cliff's current state. Maintaining the huts is hard work and in these days of no-effort package holidays not everyone would see the pleasure in holidaying there.

'Each spring we have to hack out the path to our door,' says Pip's aunt, June Stephenson. 'People who come here for the beach and the walking think it's the council that keeps the paths clear, but it's not. It's us. Once you start, however, there's always someone who'll come along and help. That's the spirit of the place.'

Because everyone knows everyone else, the children are allowed to roam more freely. 'Obviously we weren't allowed to swim without an adult watching, but it could be pretty much any adult,' recalls Pip Bond's eldest daughter, Louisa. 'If they weren't your own aunt or uncle, they'd be your neighbours, someone you'd known since you were a baby.'

On a hot summer's day, instead of being broken up by individuals staking out territory with windbreakers, the beach has the atmosphere of a tea party. And then the whole is lent an escapist, shipwrecked feel by the remains of a fishing boat called the *Chancellor,* which sank here in 1933.

'We used to use the old trawler as goal when we played football,' says Pip. 'Some of it has become part of people's huts. We've got some of the decking as our floor and one of the tenants has the anchor in the garden.'

The tenants do a fair bit of fishing, while on days when the wind is howling, cards are popular. Even when it rains, they'll probably be outside, perhaps picking blackberries or mushrooms. But possibly the main appeal for the tenants is not so much what they do as what they don't. Many talk of it as a 'spiritual place', and for all it represents a near total escape from stress. There are no phones, no television. 'The kids don't even ask for it,' says Owen Harris.

'Time's different here,' they all agree. They consider it invaluable that they forget what day it is. Sit on a patch of ground that's springy as a mattress with moss, dotted with wild violets, and a few minutes' rest on the way to the beach can spin out as you watch the changing details of the light playing on the waves as the sun begins to set over Rame Head. All this, and you realise that, here on Treninnow Cliff, you are experiencing the true meaning of leisure.

*Article by Josie Barnard © Telegraph Group Limited*

**23** What explanation is given for the way in which the community developed?

   **A** The huts have always belonged to the same families.

   **B** Permission from farmers was originally all that was required.

   **C** The families were allowed to build there for a small charge.

   **D** It arose naturally by ignoring the legal restrictions.

**24** In what way is the Wilmots' residence 'comparatively grand'?

   **A** It consists of two huts joined together.

   **B** It is more strongly built.

   **C** The furniture is impressive.

   **D** It has a magnificent view.

**25** Why are the families concerned about the change of ownership of the Cliff?

   **A** The Cliff now belongs to two different councils.

   **B** They are afraid that the council will tell them to remove the huts.

   **C** There has been an enormous increase in the rent they have to pay.

   **D** Some older owners of the huts may not be able to afford it.

**26** What general impression is given of the families' feeling about the Cliff?

   **A** They think most people nowadays are too lazy to enjoy it.

   **B** They have too much work to do to enjoy it themselves.

   **C** They think the council should be responsible for keeping it clean.

   **D** They are proud of the way they work together to preserve it.

**27** Why are children allowed more freedom here than in most places on holiday?

   **A** There is nowhere for them to go to get lost.

   **B** There is no danger to them on the cliff or the beach.

   **C** Parents trust their neighbours to keep an eye on them.

   **D** Parents take it in turns to watch them.

**28** What has happened to the fishing boat that was wrecked there?

   **A** Most of it is now under the water.

   **B** Children play games in it.

   **C** It has been useful in furnishing the huts.

   **D** It is still used for fishing in fine weather.

**29** What does the writer suggest is 'the true meaning of leisure'?

   **A** going a long way from home

   **B** having nothing to do all day

   **C** getting away from the worries of modern life

   **D** feeling at ease in natural surroundings

**Part 1**

For questions 1–18, read the texts and decide which answer (**A**, **B**, **C** or **D**) best fits each gap.

## MIXING SPORT AND POLITICS

The Prime Minister of Australia, Mr Howard, is a keen supporter of national teams. But since his victory in the recent elections, his constant (1) .............. at sporting events has been counter-productive. In the past month, Australia have been defeated at rugby by England, the ultimate (2) .............. , and beaten by France in the final of the Davis Cup at tennis. Mr Howard sat through all three days of the Davis Cup debacle and in some spectators' view, got the (3) .............. for it.

Anyone who has ever (4) .............. with Australians knows they are just going through a temporary bad (5) .............. , but until they start winning again, Mr Howard will need to (6) .............. his head down.

| | | | | | | | | |
|---|---|---|---|---|---|---|---|---|
| 1 | **A** | residence | **B** | attendance | **C** | occupation | **D** | assistance |
| 2 | **A** | shame | **B** | disgrace | **C** | blot | **D** | smear |
| 3 | **A** | blame | **B** | fault | **C** | guilt | **D** | charge |
| 4 | **A** | competed | **B** | contested | **C** | opposed | **D** | matched |
| 5 | **A** | course | **B** | spot | **C** | patch | **D** | hole |
| 6 | **A** | put | **B** | pull | **C** | hold | **D** | keep |

## A HOME FOR SANTA CLAUS

According to legend, Santa Claus, or Father Christmas, lives at the North Pole but as this is inaccessible to tourists, a number of countries (7) .............. with each other for the honour of being his home. Finland has a stronger (8) .............. than its rivals because Santa's reindeer come from its northern province of Lapland, though visitors may be rather (9) .............. to find them not pulling his sleigh but as an item on the (10) .............. in the restaurant at Santa Village. Meanwhile, Sweden is promoting Santaworld as his true home, and Iceland and Greenland are both trying to get in on the (11) .............. , despite the disadvantage for the (12) .............. of a total absence of reindeer and for the latter of 85% of the country being covered in ice.

| | | | | | | | | |
|---|---|---|---|---|---|---|---|---|
| 7 | **A** | combat | **B** | contest | **C** | conflict | **D** | vie |
| 8 | **A** | claim | **B** | right | **C** | merit | **D** | demand |
| 9 | **A** | set off | **B** | put out | **C** | let down | **D** | shaken up |
| 10 | **A** | meal | **B** | fare | **C** | card | **D** | menu |
| 11 | **A** | act | **B** | scene | **C** | performance | **D** | show |
| 12 | **A** | prior | **B** | earlier | **C** | former | **D** | first |

**PROSPECTS POOR FOR SKIERS**

Global warming is being cited as the (13) .............. for the slow start to this year's European ski season. At a time when resorts should be making the final preparations for visitors, the mildest autumn in (14) .............. memory has given way to (15) .............. rain, closing down almost all of the lifts. A leading expert in Switzerland has warned that within 15 years the (16) .............. -lying ski resorts in the Alps may be surrounded by green fields throughout the winter. Trying hard to look on the (17) .............. side, however, a representative of the British Ski Club remarked that falls of snow are so unpredictable that the situation could change (18) .............. in the next few days.

| | | | | | | | |
|---|---|---|---|---|---|---|---|
| 13 | **A** offender | **B** culprit | **C** respondent | **D** suspect |
| 14 | **A** existing | **B** current | **C** contemporary | **D** living |
| 15 | **A** stormy | **B** tempestuous | **C** streaming | **D** torrential |
| 16 | **A** low | **B** level | **C** deep | **D** flat |
| 17 | **A** bright | **B** good | **C** positive | **D** favourable |
| 18 | **A** basically | **B** wholly | **C** radically | **D** essentially |

## *Vocabulary Development*

Complete the sentences below with a word or phrase taken from the choices for the questions you have answered. The sentences are printed in the same order as the questions. Note the difference between the correct answer below and a phrase of similar meaning in the passages above.

1    The captain said the ................................. they received from their coach was vital to their success.

2    It would be a terrible ................................. on their record to lose to England.

3    The spectators thought it was the Prime Minister's ................................. that they lost.

4    The defendant's account is bound to ................................. with his accuser's.

5    I wouldn't like to see reindeer on the bill of ................................. at a restaurant.

6    If Santa Claus was really Saint Nicholas, none of these countries could claim to be the ................................. of his birth.

7    We don't really know what is responsible for the lack of snow but global warming appears to be the prime ................................. .

8    You'll find the latest information about ski resorts in the ................................. issue of this magazine.

9    It's dangerous to take a boat out in ................................. weather.

10    Don't give up hope. Try to adopt a more ................................. attitude.

## Part 2

These two texts are concerned with leisure activities. For questions 19–22, choose the answer (**A, B, C** or **D**) which you think fits best according to the text.

### DAY TRIPS FOR FAMILIES

The Isle of Wight is the dinosaur capital of Britain. **Dinosaur Isle** opens in August and combines dinosaur models and fossil walks with the opportunity to analyse remains.
*Adults £4.60, children (3-16) £2.60*

Make a splash at the country's first indoor water rollercoaster, with over 100 metres of ups and downs before you drop into the pool at **Waterworld Park**.
*Adults £5.50, children (5-14) £4.99*

The **Harbour Promenade** is ideal for kids who like things to go with a bang. The attraction shows what life is like in the navy and there is an interactive exhibition featuring famous battles.
*Adults £4.00, children (6-16) £2.40*

Stagestruck children can sing along with the cast of *Chicago* and learn dances from them during **Kids Week** at the end of August. Children can see a show for free if accompanied by an adult.
*Free for kids.*

Gloucester Cathedral featured in the first Harry Potter film, and nearby there is **The Birds of Prey Centre**, with every kind of owl Potter addicts could wish for.
*Adults £5.75, children (4-16) £3.50*

At **Folly Farm** new additions include wallabies. Children can cuddle rabbits and chipmunks at the pet centre or thrill to the grace of a display with falcons. And there is an indoor funfair to visit, too.
*Adults £3.95, children (3-15) £2.95*

**Steam Dreams** gives you the chance to prove to your children that there was a time when travelling by train in Britain was a pleasure. The service connects with the country's historic cities.
*£39.50 return fare, food extra*

Take a chance on the weather and visit the beautiful **Open Air Theatre** in Regents Park. A special show for children, *Pinocchio*, runs throughout August, and you can combine it with a visit to the London Zoo.
*Tickets are £8.00*

**19** Harry has two sons, Tim, aged 11, and Eric, aged 9. Tim is interested in history, but Eric just likes excitement. Where should Harry take them?

    **A**  Dinosaur Isle

    **B**  Waterworld Park

    **C**  Harbour Promenade

    **D**  Steam Dreams

**20** Jane has two daughters, Emma, aged 14, and Margaret, aged 12. Emma is keen to go onto the stage when she grows up, while Margaret wants to be a naturalist. Where should Jane take them?

    **A**  Kids Week

    **B**  The Birds of Prey Centre

    **C**  Folly Farm

    **D**  Open Air Theatre

## THE IMPORTANCE OF TELEVISION

For the first time in living memory, viewing figures indicate that the BBC has replaced Independent Television as the channel most watched in Britain. This will no doubt be a cause of satisfaction to the Director, Greg Dyke, whose obsession this has been since he was appointed. But it offers no cause for rejoicing to the rest of us. In effect, the BBC went all out to attract the lowest common denominator among audiences. Soap operas, chat shows and mindless games dominate the screen at prime time, and one has to stay up late to see anything of educational value.

Unlike the state television services in other countries the BBC does not bombard viewers with advertisements (except for its own products!). But it is only able to do without advertising because viewers are compelled by law to pay over £100 a year for a licence to watch television, whether they watch the BBC's programmes or are permanently tuned to their rivals.

If measured by the number of hours spent watching it, television is the most popular leisure activity in the country. It has enormous power to broaden people's horizons. At one time the justification for the licence fee was that the BBC provided this invaluable service. But in my view, it has forfeited that right by the means it has employed in its relentless pursuit of larger audiences.

**21**  What is the main accusation that the writer is making against the BBC?

   **A**  That it is only concerned with the number of viewers.

   **B**  That it has sacrificed quality for quantity.

   **C**  That the best programmes are shown at night.

   **D**  That it charges too much for its programmes.

**22**  Why does the writer consider that the BBC has no right to charge a licence fee?

   **A**  Because it advertises its own programmes.

   **B**  Because people would rather watch other channels.

   **C**  Because it no longer fulfils its responsibility to the public.

   **D**  Because its programmes are vulgar.

---

**Active Vocabulary List**

These are some words and phrases closely connected with the subject of leisure. If you are not sure of the meaning of any words or phrases, look them up in your dictionary.

*watch TV/a video, listen to music*      *read, play computer games*
*go to the cinema/a concert/a club/a café*      *go shopping*
*go to the beach/the park/the country*      *go jogging/go for a walk/run*
*go out for a meal, have a picnic*      *have a party/a barbecue*

## Part 3 (Ordering paragraphs)

This article consists of 15 paragraphs. Seven of them have been removed. Choose from the paragraphs **A-H** the one that fits each gap (**23-29**). There is one extra paragraph that does not fit and which you do not need to use.

## MOTORCYCLE MENACE IN NATIONAL PARKS

Motorcyclists riding at high speeds in national parks and terrorising other road users in unofficial 'time trials' have become such a menace that a police helicopter is being deployed to catch offenders.

**23**

In the Peak District National Park, Derbyshire Police have deployed the force helicopter for the first time above winding stretches of roads to catch speeding bikers. Notorious sections include the A6 between Buxton and Matlock Bath, where motorcyclists participate in time trials. Notices have now been posted along the road warning riders that the helicopter is monitoring their movements.

**24**

This attitude was underlined by an article in a magazine for bikers which has even road-tested high-performance machines in Snowdonia and extolled the virtues of using them between isolated beauty spots. The pleas of wardens not to promote the area for high-speed riding were ignored and the article referred with pride to 'sheep fleeing for their lives' and to the engine noise 'shattering the serenity.'

**25**

In the Yorkshire Dales, hundreds of riders follow an unofficial timed run known as the 'Dales TT' from Leeds and Bradford to Devil's Bridge. Police using radar traps last month booked up to 150 motorcycles speeding on the A65 Settle by-pass as part of the time trials.

**26**

Residents in the Dales have complained that the tranquillity of the area is being ruined as the motorcyclists ride at great speeds along winding roads through villages in Ribblesdale and Wensleydale. Speeding is also a serious problem on the road between Garsdale Head and Kirkby Stephen, where farmers have complained that the raucous machines are frightening animals and deterring tourists.

**27**

The route the riders have chosen not only angers residents but takes a gruesome toll of the riders themselves. An increasing number of small shrines, decked with flowers, mark the spots where riders have been killed.

**28**

Mr Fenten also wants the police to use more radar speed guns on minor roads. 'Bikers are ruining the peace and quiet of the area but nobody is actively discouraging them from riding through the park.'

**29**

Residents wonder whether it will have any more effect than the Bike 2000 Campaign the police introduced to persuade motorcyclists to ride more responsibly. Accidents were reduced slightly but it had only limited effects on speeds and noise levels.

*Article by Andrew Morgan © Telegraph Group Limited*

**A** 'It is utterly horrendous,' he said. 'Many tourists have decided against staying in the Horton area. We want tougher moves to discourage bikers from travelling at speed, including a stronger police presence, and we want them kept on peripheral trunk roads.'

**B** Many more might have been caught but to avoid detection, riders are taking minor roads through the Dales and alerting each other with mobile telephones to sightings of the police.

**C** Other problem areas include roads from Buxton to Macclesfield and Ashbourne, where the helicopter will be used to alert ground patrols to dangerous driving. A police motorcyclist from the area said: 'These roads are winding and hilly and bikers get pleasure from that kind of road.'

**D** The problem has grown rapidly in the past decade with the rise in the popularity of motorcycles. It is worst at weekends but many motorcycle clubs ride out from the cities on summer evenings. In consequence, Horton in Ribblesdale's parish council decided last week to press for urgent talks with the police, demanding a 40 mph (64 km/h) speed limit on all non-trunk roads in the Dales.

**E** On the Isle of Wight, joyriders on motorcycles are terrorising a tiger sanctuary. The sanctuary's owner said he was regularly kept awake into the early hours of the morning by the animals moaning in fear after being terrified by the illegal racing and revving of engines.

**F** Riders are attracted to mountain roads in the Peak District, Snowdonia and the Yorkshire Dales, where they enjoy the thrill of putting motorcycles capable of speeds of up to 150 miles per hour (240 km/h) through their paces.

**G** According to Wilf Fenten, a parish councillor for Horton in Ribblesdale, at least 700 motorcycles were counted on a single Saturday passing through the village. In the last week of June, up to 200 riders were recorded in the village on one morning alone.

**H** Park officials have complained to the magazine about the article, pointing out that 13 motorcyclists were killed, 49 seriously injured and 151 slightly injured in 1999 on the same roads. The park also alerted the police to the article. The police have now issued speed warning notices on a notorious 30-mile (48 km) stretch in the south of the park but, according to wardens, the notices have had little effect.

*Part I*

For questions 1–18, read the texts and decide which answer (**A**, **B**, **C** or **D**) best fits each gap.

**THE EURO SYMBOL**

Taxpayers in Europe are in debt to Jean-Pierre Malivoir. Instead of (1) ............... a host of highly paid designers to (2) ............... ideas for a symbol for the euro, this European Commission official (3) ............... to work and got the job done for nothing.

The symbol had to be immediately recognisable and easy to write. The eventual design slipped through without much discussion at a meeting that had been (4) ............... to discuss other issues. Perhaps as much by (5) ............... as judgement, Malivoir's design achieved instant acceptance. Like many successful symbols, it was very simple. It was inspired by the Greek letter epsilon, with two simple horizontal lines (6) ............... it.

| 1 | **A** charging | **B** commissioning | **C** entrusting | **D** electing |
|---|---|---|---|---|
| 2 | **A** bring about | **B** come up with | **C** give rise to | **D** make up |
| 3 | **A** put | **B** sent | **C** came | **D** set |
| 4 | **A** collected | **B** congregated | **C** convened | **D** assembled |
| 5 | **A** chance | **B** accident | **C** fortune | **D** luck |
| 6 | **A** drawn across | **B** drawn around | **C** written across | **D** written around |

**KNOWING WHEN TO GO**

Fans are generally taken (7) ............... when a famous actor or actress suddenly (8) ............... the profession at the height of his or her career. Greta Garbo, who made her last film when she was not yet 40, was a notable (9) ............... in point.

Sportsmen and women face this decision earliest. Though they generally have evidence that their powers are in (10) ............... , very few have the self-awareness to get out while the going is still (11) ............... .

Politicians are perhaps the last to realise that the game is up. As long as they can (12) ............... on to power, they refuse to accept the advice of party members, no doubt suspecting that it is prompted by their colleagues' own ambitions!

| 7 | **A** surprised | **B** astonished | **C** unawares | **D** unexpected |
|---|---|---|---|---|
| 8 | **A** quits | **B** withdraws | **C** resigns | **D** vacates |
| 9 | **A** case | **B** type | **C** example | **D** illustration |
| 10 | **A** decrease | **B** decline | **C** descent | **D** decay |
| 11 | **A** fine | **B** well | **C** good | **D** fair |
| 12 | **A** keep | **B** stick | **C** fasten | **D** hang |

### SHOULD WE TRUST THE EXPERTS?

As usual, the gurus of the stock market are making their (13) .............. for the coming year, but this year their air of infallibility may not be enough to (14) .............. their dismal failure last time. Not one of them correctly forecast that the market would (15) .............. rather than rise. The main reason for this is that they are naturally biased in favour of expansion, partly because, by the (16) .............. of averages, shares tend to rise but also because they have a personal interest in being optimistic. If the stock market is (17) .............. , they can expect a bonus; if it falls through the (18) .............. , their jobs may go with it. They would like us to believe that things can only get better.

| | | | | | | | |
|---|---|---|---|---|---|---|---|
| 13 | **A** expectations | **B** predictions | **C** presentiments | **D** warnings |
| 14 | **A** dress | **B** cloak | **C** bury | **D** cover |
| 15 | **A** fade | **B** drop | **C** fall | **D** sink |
| 16 | **A** norm | **B** rule | **C** code | **D** law |
| 17 | **A** booming | **B** busting | **C** rocking | **D** jumping |
| 18 | **A** ground | **B** bottom | **C** floor | **D** foot |

## Vocabulary Development

Complete the sentences below with a word or phrase taken from the choices for the questions you have answered. The sentences are printed in the same order as the questions. Note the difference between the correct answer below and a phrase of similar meaning in the passages above.

1   Instead of .................................. the design to experts, Malivoir did it himself.

2   We did not expect the decision to join the euro would .................................. so much heated argument.

3   A circle had been .................................. the correct answer.

4   No member of this government ever .................................. from his post, admitting his mistakes.

5   Greta Garbo set an .................................. by retiring at the height of her fame.

6   None of them will ever give up power so long as they can .................................. hold of it.

7   Their forecasts last year were disappointing and did not come up to .................................. .

8   The memory of the terrible Wall Street Crash of 1929 will never .................................. .

9   As a general .................................. , shares tend to rise in value.

10  The most successful investors are those who guess the point when the market has hit .................................. and can only go up.

## Part 2

These two texts are concerned with different aspects of business. For questions **19–22**, choose the answer (**A**, **B**, **C** or **D**) which you think fits best according to the text.

### TURNING ON THE CHARM

Charm was originally a feminine weapon, used by women like Cleopatra, compelled to employ it on men when brute force would not serve their turn. But women do not enjoy a monopoly of it in the modern world in business or politics, and both then and now charm has very little to do with passion and a great deal with obtaining power over others. The foremost political charmer of our times is ex-President Clinton, a man with a monumental ego who nevertheless has the ability to get people to like him.

The technique charmers need to employ depends first of all on being a good listener; most people want to talk about themselves and are captivated by someone with a ready, sympathetic smile. All that the charmers need is a good line in amusing conversation. Now and again, it pays to play hard-to-get, especially if you are a beautiful girl, pursued by many admirers. But the end product, whether you want people to vote for you, lend you money, buy your product, or merely marry you, is the same. Turn on the charm and watch them become putty in your hands.

19   What is the main point that the writer is making in the first paragraph?

A   Those who are weak must use charm in order to persuade.

B   Charm is an emotional tool, more suitable for women.

C   Those who set out to charm others aim to gain control over them.

D   Charming people are invariably dishonest.

20   What is the basis of the charmers' success in the writer's opinion?

A   People believe the charmers are interested in them.

B   They let people talk instead of talking about themselves.

C   They are very entertaining to talk to.

D   They encourage people to run after them.

*The following are taken from recommendations in newspapers on which shares readers ought to buy and sell.*

### Engineering Inco

Now that the company has clarified its commercial plans, we can expect a rise in share value of up to 25%, regaining most of this year's lost ground.

### Davidson's Bank

The bank's recent statement was 'mildly positive', which is some comfort for shareholders battered by this year's fall. This should enable them to claw back 10%.

### Amalgamated Tobacco

Over the last 25 years, Amalgamated has consistently out-performed the market and this is likely to continue. An excellent 'hedge' against declining profits elsewhere.

### Harris, Jones and Thompson

Profits have fallen 11% and trade in the hotel sector is still erratic. Prospects for the brewing division are more promising, and this may offset losses in other areas.

### TGN Breweries

The firm is in a dilemma because of its dual focus as brewer and large-scale operator of pubs. Selling off surplus capacity will not halt the downward trend.

### International Pancras

Turnover has increased by 7.2% this year, following a strong performance by many divisions. Its forecast for the coming year remains unchanged and should be met.

### QJT Group

Interim results were in line with expectations. But many contracts have been cancelled because of a decline in the area as a whole which has closed down rivals. A good buy if it survives.

### OnLineCo

The recent acquisition of PaulCo was trumpeted to the world but will add little to group revenues. Worth holding onto but hardly a safe bet for the future.

**21**  If you were looking for a safe investment for the future, which share would you buy?

  **A**  Engineering Inco

  **B**  Amalgamated Tobacco

  **C**  International Pancras

  **D**  QJT Group

**22**  If you had made a reasonable profit on the shares, which share would you be wise to sell?

  **A**  Davidson's Bank

  **B**  Harris, Jones and Thompson

  **C**  TGN Breweries

  **D**  OnLineCo

### Active Vocabulary List

These are some words and phrases closely connected with the subject of business. If you are not sure of the meaning of any words or phrases, look them up in your dictionary.

*business, trade, industry*
*company/firm, Ltd, plc*
*deal, agreement, contract*
*manage, run, set up*

*commerce, merchandise*
*corporation, multinational, subsidiary*
*businessman/woman, entrepreneur*
*small, family business*

## Part 3 (Multiple-choice comprehension)

Read this account about the way in which politicians use dogs to assist them in their campaigns. For questions **23–29**, choose the answer (**A**, **B**, **C** or **D**) which you think fits best according to the text.

### HOUNDED INTO OFFICE

As our would-be rulers snap and snarl at one another's heels during an election campaign, spare a thought for their four-legged friends. For in the desperate need to herd us toward the election booths, even family pets must become political animals. Not content with kissing babies, bombarding our homes with junk mail and accosting the confused and unemployed in shopping precincts, aspiring MPs may well have the family pooch in tow on the hustings, hoping some of its qualities of loyalty, devotion and all-round lovableness might rub off. According to sociologists, such hopes are not misplaced. Apparently we do attach positive social attributes to pet owners. They are seen as trustworthy, kind-hearted and generous to the vulnerable.

[1]Tony Blair is no pet lover – he notoriously expelled [2]John Major's cat, Humphrey, from Downing Street in 1997, prompting rumours that he had gone so far as to have the hapless moggy bumped off. But it can be no coincidence that he chose to announce the election date from the stage of a South London comprehensive school, giving television cameras heart-warming visuals that included a cross, a school choir singing hymns, and [3]David Blunkett's guide dog, Lucy. This faithful, intelligent, supremely reliable black Labrador-retriever cross has come to symbolise for the public the same sterling qualities her blind owner showed as Education Secretary.

When New Labour came to power in 1997, Mr Blunkett was regarded with some suspicion as an off-message Northern relic of old Labour. His Braille machine and Lucy's dog box were the only modest personal touches he brought to his Westminster office. Then, to the delight of children, he started to take his guide dog on school visits, using tests about her age to assess the success of his numeracy policy. He also uses Lucy as a foil for his political jokes, interpreting her sleepiness, or on one occasion her vomiting while he was being attacked in Parliament, as responses to the shortcomings of his opponents' debating skills.

No one could have played the canine card more often than [4]Peter Mandelson. During the 1997 campaign, he hired a bulldog called Fitz, perhaps to focus voters' minds on New Labour's patriotic qualities. But Fitz was so ugly, belligerent and bowlegged that pictures of him had to be airbrushed to soften him up.

Mandelson next tried to sell us a pup with the far cuter Bobby, a retriever. Yet photographs of Bobby enthusiastically licking his master's face and stories about the minor cult status he had won in Northern Ireland and the valentines he was sent by other dogs failed to make his saturnine master appear lovable. Even adding a second dog, a Jack Russell called Jack, did not do the trick. Both dogs have now been removed from the national limelight, along with their owner, to try to win the love of the voters of Hartlepool. Mandelson's eventual downfall was prefigured in 1999 when Bobby went for an inaugural tour of Parliament and was cornered by Lucy. Lucy made short work of the new dog on the block. As Blunkett put it afterwards: 'Lucy growled and saw him off. She showed him who's boss around here.'

America, even more than Britain, is the land of pet spin, though it can occasionally backfire. President Lyndon B Johnson lifted one of his beagles, Him and Her, by its long floppy ears during a photo shoot. He denied being unkind, saying that his mother had always picked him up by his ears, but the public outcry sent his popularity plummeting. But the dog in the White House has a long history, from George Washington, who kept a dog, a parrot and a horse, right through to George W Bush's spaniel, Spot, who has just moved in.

Richard Nixon had mixed results in pet politics. As Eisenhower's vice-presidential candidate in 1952, he managed to help the electorate overlook his five o'clock shadow and somewhat repellent personality by parading his spaniel, Checkers. The trick didn't work twice. In 1973, as he faced impeachment, Nixon tried to soften his image again with a new dog, the Irish setter, King Timahoe, who shook hands with everyone. But master and man never hit it off. On one of the White House tapes, as Nixon complained that his aides were deserting him, a dog barks and the President bellows: 'King! Goddam! Get off me!'

Tony Blair is unlikely to follow the American example too enthusiastically, and he would be wise to remember both the example of Peter Mandelson and the words of Mark Twain: 'Heaven goes by favour. If it went by merit, you would stay out and your dog would go in.'

---

[1] the Prime Minister; [2] the previous Prime Minister; [3] then Minister of Education, since appointed Home Secretary; [4] former Minister for Northern Ireland, obliged to resign

*Article by Vanora Bennet, © The Times*

**23**  Which of these words in the first paragraph does not describe a politician's pet?

  **A**  snap

  **B**  snarl

  **C**  herd

  **D**  pooch

**24**  Why do politicians make use of dogs in their political campaigns?

  **A**  Because they know we all love animals.

  **B**  Because we don't bother to read their addresses to us.

  **C**  Because they help us to remember them.

  **D**  Because they hope we will think they are like them.

**25**  What is the writer saying in the second paragraph about the Prime Minister's attitude to animals?

  **A**  He is fond of dogs but does not like cats.

  **B**  He had a cat destroyed because it belonged to his opponent.

  **C**  He saw the political advantage of appearing with Mr Blunkett's dog.

  **D**  He does not like pets but made an exception of Lucy because she was useful to her owner.

**26**  How did Lucy prove most useful to her owner politically?

  **A**  She made people feel sorry for him.

  **B**  She enabled him to transform his public image.

  **C**  She helped him to form his educational policy.

  **D**  She gave him the chance to insult his opponents.

**27**  Why was Mr Mandelson unsuccessful in making use of dogs politically?

  **A**  They did not convince the electors that he was patriotic.

  **B**  They did not convince the electors that he was like them.

  **C**  They were only of interest locally.

  **D**  They fell foul of Mr Blunkett's dog.

**28**  What was President Johnson's error in using dogs?

  **A**  He appeared to treat them cruelly.

  **B**  He treated them in the same way as his mother had treated him.

  **C**  He made a silly excuse for using them.

  **D**  He used them far too often.

**29**  And where did President Nixon go wrong?

  **A**  He had not shaved when he was photographed with his dog.

  **B**  They failed to disguise his unpleasant personality.

  **C**  The second dog irritated his colleagues.

  **D**  The second dog betrayed his real personality.

## Part 1

For questions 1–18, read the texts and decide which answer (**A**, **B**, **C** or **D**) best fits each gap.

### BLOOD

Blood is not only essential to our physical well-being but has always possessed great imaginative significance. The notion that you can have too much of it (1) .............. people to be bled, sometimes to death, by (2) .............. doctors.

Royal families like the Hapsburgs (3) .............. it into their heads that theirs was too (4) .............. to share with lesser (5) .............. and kept it in the family by marrying exclusively with each other. This produced such features as the notorious Hapsburg jaw, which led to the Spanish Hapsburg line (6) .............. out.

| 1 | **A** caused | **B** made | **C** provoked | **D** contributed |
|---|---|---|---|---|
| 2 | **A** unconscious | **B** unaware | **C** illiterate | **D** ignorant |
| 3 | **A** put | **B** got | **C** fixed | **D** set |
| 4 | **A** precious | **B** priceless | **C** unique | **D** valued |
| 5 | **A** stocks | **B** species | **C** breeds | **D** races |
| 6 | **A** dropping | **B** dying | **C** passing | **D** falling |

### JUNK FOOD

A recent survey suggests that the health of 20% of British adults is seriously at (7) .............. because they are overweight. The increase in obesity is due to people eating more and using less energy, and junk food undoubtedly (8) .............. its part. According to one theory, we eat too much because food was (9) .............. in the past, and we (10) .............. up for it when it was plentiful, but this is no longer necessary.

A recent publication in the USA suggests that dieting and exercise are not enough to cure obesity. The (11) .............. of obesity there makes people complacent. We need to compare ourselves with others and feel dissatisfied to lose weight. A visit to a third-world country, taking (12) .............. of what we saw, might do the trick.

| 7 | **A** stake | **B** risk | **C** danger | **D** threat |
|---|---|---|---|---|
| 8 | **A** acts | **B** serves | **C** plays | **D** contributes |
| 9 | **A** rare | **B** missing | **C** scarce | **D** thin |
| 10 | **A** made | **B** filled | **C** took | **D** used |
| 11 | **A** commonness | **B** generalisation | **C** presence | **D** prevalence |
| 12 | **A** attention | **B** note | **C** regard | **D** shame |

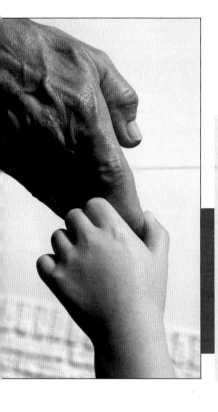

### FREE HANDS

Some people claim that their hands seem to have (13) ............... of their own. In a few cases, when someone's brain has been damaged, the left and right hands may act independently, and one, for example, may (14) ............... what the other has just done up. If this were the case in (15) ............... circumstances, it would provide a wonderful excuse for students making rude gestures instead of (16) ............... up their hands to ask a question, not to (17) ............... for people accused of theft or strangling.

The law only accepts such defence when medical evidence has been provided. Schizophrenics whose hands commit violent acts may be (18) ............... as ill rather than wicked, unlike those whose evil actions are premeditated.

| 13 | **A** a wish | **B** an intention | **C** a will | **D** a tendency |
|----|----|----|----|----|
| 14 | **A** disjoin | **B** detach | **C** release | **D** unfasten |
| 15 | **A** common | **B** average | **C** conventional | **D** normal |
| 16 | **A** raising | **B** putting | **C** lifting | **D** setting |
| 17 | **A** notice | **B** mention | **C** remark | **D** include |
| 18 | **A** treated | **B** considered | **C** estimated | **D** pronounced |

## Vocabulary Development

Complete the sentences below with a word or phrase taken from the choices for the questions you have answered. The sentences are printed in the same order as the questions. Note the difference between the correct answer below and a phrase of similar meaning in the passages above.

1   Recent political events have shown that you can ................................... people believe anything if they want to believe it.

2   There is something wrong with the reading programmes in schools if there are more ................................... people now than there were 100 years ago.

3   What ................................... that idea into your head?

4   There is only one in existence, so it is ................................... .

5   If people are seriously overweight, their health is in ................................... .

6   Overeating and lack of exercise both ................................... to obesity.

7   If they ate less, paying ................................... to their diet, they would be healthier.

8   They have decided to ................................... him from prison immediately.

9   It's ................................... knowledge that the Prime Minister intervened on his behalf.

10   They are ................................... up a committee to investigate the problem.

*Part 2*

These two texts are concerned with health. For questions **19–22**, choose the answer (**A**, **B**, **C** or **D**) which you think fits best according to the text.

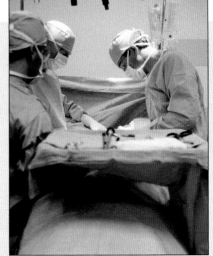

### ONCE 'THE ENVY OF THE WORLD'

There was a time when the National Health Service, perhaps only in its own opinion, was regarded as one that other countries envied. But it has long since fallen in public esteem to the point where less than half of those answering a recent questionnaire were satisfied with the standard of care it offered and 50% doubted whether the local hospital would be capable of carrying out an operation on the day it was booked.

By this time, nearly five years after being elected, the Government can no longer blame the state of affairs on its predecessors as it has been wont to do. Up to now it has been so obsessed with such statistics as the number of people waiting for operations that it has encouraged hospitals to fudge the figures without this having any noticeable effect. It has taken all this time for its publicists to realise that what matters is not how many people there are in the queue but how long any of them has to wait.

On the whole, patients are reasonably satisfied with their doctors. The problem starts when they have to go to hospital. It might help to change the popular view of hospitals if a little more time and energy were spent on their appearance. Entering a place supposed to be concerned with your health which hasn't seen a coat of paint in years is bound to colour one's attitude to the whole set-up. But ministers who only care about manipulated statistics are unlikely to spend money on something that cannot be quantified.

**19**   What is the main point of the writer's argument in the first two paragraphs?

   **A**   That the National Health Service is no longer the best in the world.

   **B**   That people do not trust the Service to look after them properly.

   **C**   That previous governments were mainly responsible for its problems.

   **D**   That the present government is more concerned with appearances than with improving the situation.

**20**   What is the writer saying about hospitals in the last paragraph?

   **A**   Doctors cannot do their job properly if they are forced to rely on them.

   **B**   First impressions count more than politicians realise.

   **C**   The standards of cleanliness in hospitals are disgusting.

   **D**   It is not worth cleaning them up because it does not win votes.

## SO WHAT'S YOUR PHOBIA?

Almost all of us have unreasonable fears. It's no good telling some people that spiders are harmless, or that planes do not crash very often and passengers do not suffocate in tube trains in normal circumstances. In such situations, whichever fear is uppermost, the tell-tale symptoms appear. Their hands begin to sweat, their hearts to thump: they are trying desperately not to faint or scream or betray their embarrassment. The tendency has been for others to be unsympathetic. 'Don't be silly,' they say, and dismiss the subject. But in fact there is usually a rational basis for such fears and the way to deal with them is to learn to live with them.

My phobia, for example, relates to heights. When I cross a bridge over the motorway near my home which has a low parapet, I struggle with the temptation to throw myself over it onto the passing traffic. A friend explained to me that because I am very tall and the parapet does not reach my waist, my balance is disturbed. Since then, I have crossed the bridge with my eyes firmly fixed on the footpath in front of me.

Spiders? Well, the experts say: 'talk about them, draw them, look at pictures of them or videos, convince yourself that they are really no danger to you. You are not a fly.' It sounds like a good solution. But don't try to get me to talk about rats. They really are dangerous to health, and avoiding them is just common sense!

**21**   What is the writer saying about phobias in the first paragraph?

   **A**   Only a few unfortunate people suffer from them.

   **B**   They can be solved if people are told that they are not justified.

   **C**   They are entirely a mental process.

   **D**   They can be overcome if you come to terms with them.

**22**   The writer believes his own phobias

   **A**   disappeared once he was given an explanation for them.

   **B**   can only be cured by fixing the mind on something else.

   **C**   would be cured if he talked about them to others who do not have them.

   **D**   are not really phobias at all, but natural reactions.

### Active Vocabulary List

These are some words and phrases commonly connected with the subject of health. If you are not sure of the meaning of any words or phrases, look them up in your dictionary.

| | |
|---|---|
| examination, treatment, cure | conventional/alternative medicine |
| injection, operation, surgery | acupuncture, herbal remedy |
| X-ray, physiotherapy | medication, dose, prescription |
| surgery, clinic, hospital | casualty, emergency |
| diet, low-fat, high-fibre | home cooking, fast food, microwave |

## Part 3 (Ordering paragraphs)

This article consists of 15 paragraphs. Seven of them have been removed. Choose from the paragraphs **A-H** the one that fits each gap (**23-29**). There is one extra paragraph that does not fit and which you do not need to use.

### TESTING THE WATER: DO SPAS WORK?

Last winter was awful. I spent most of it in bed, suffering from one chest infection after another. Ever since I became run down after thyroid collapse and pneumonia, I have had chest trouble and I would love to do something about it.

**23**

Then Thermalia, which specialises in health tourism, came up with the offer of a week at Termes Montbrio in Spain. They offer a programme for improving 'respiratory tracks' and I couldn't resist the idea of reading books in the Mediterranean sunshine and thinking of my husband struggling to get the children to school. Thermalia specialises in spas that purport to do you good. As Miro Sajfert, the managing director, explained, most spas are old-fashioned, and adopt a utilitarian, even bossy, approach.

**24**

Miro passed me a pile of research papers, mainly from the University of Padua, where the denizens of the department of biology wallow in the natural hot springs of Abano Terme. Their aim is to prove to the medical establishment that treatments (fangotherapy) using local mud impregnated and matured in that water are more beneficial than using any old mud.

**25**

Scientists believe that the mineral content of the spring and the algae in mud imbued in it have an impact that lasts for months after a visit. As the Paduans show, mineral waters, whether drunk or wallowed in, penetrate the tissues and alter hormone levels.

**26**

One problem for spa users is that European Spas Association members cannot even agree on the definition of a spa. Is a health farm in England offering true thalassotherapy when it imports sea water for a treatment pool? Can an inner-city beauty salon with fancy showers call itself a spa?

**27**

Water is relaxing to be in or near and relaxation benefits the immune system and lessens arterial narrowing. At thalassotherapy centres, the sea air, with its high ozone content, reinforces this effect. At inland spas, it is often the sunshine and the clean air that make a difference. Accounts by 18th and 19th century visitors to spas convinced Kavounas that the 'cures' owed most to a light diet and drinking water instead of alcohol.

**28**

My week in Spain involved an hour and a half of therapy each day, in three sections. Part one consisted of breathing in mineral-enriched steam to soften the bronchial tissues. Next came oxygen treatment, lying in a chair breathing from a bubbling cylinder to reoxygenate those cells deprived over the winter by my poor breathing.

**29**

I emerged after a week feeling and looking considerably better. But I cannot tell what made the difference. Was it the treatment itself, the change of scene and pace, the water, or the absence of all responsibility? Also, I cannot tell whether my lungs benefited. If asthma was my problem, I would know whether I was breathing more easily, but how do you know if you are less likely to succumb to another infection? I'll find out next winter.

*Article by Cassandra Jardine © Telegraph Group Limited*

**A**  The same holds true today. And yet, if you are visiting a spa because you have a health problem, choose with care. The hotter the water, the longer it has been underground and the higher its mineral content. Heat suits some problems and not others. Climate makes a difference. And so does the medical expertise a spa develops through long association with a particular ailment. Sometimes, too, a place is worth visiting for its doctors.

**B**  These treatments have been taken seriously in Europe since Greek and Roman times. You can get spa treatments courtesy of the state and health insurers in France, Austria, Hungary and Italy; the problem for those governments is rationing the length and frequency of the visits. Many of the springs, as at Lourdes, have acquired quasi-magical reputations for curing people. Today spas only claim to be able to help with muscular, skeletal, respiratory, digestive, skin and reproductive problems, but that's good enough for most of us!

**C**  Part three involved, on alternate days, reflexology and back massage with gentle thumping to loosen any gunk in the lungs. In addition, there were endless exercise and relaxation classes, which I attended religiously, and meals that were healthy, but not austerely so.

**D**  The deal was that I took it seriously and went for a week. 'Any less, and it won't work,' he told me firmly. He goes to a spa himself four times a year – by these he means a resort using naturally occurring spring or sea water for healing – and he believes it helps him to stay healthy.

**E**  It's not so improbable. Nicotine patches work, as Alice Kavounas, author of *Water Pure Therapy* points out, so why shouldn't bathing in fresh or sea water have an effect beneath the skin? 'They walk racehorses in the sea to strengthen them and not just for the salt,' she says. 'In Greece, people swim daily for their health.'

**F**  Britain has largely missed out on the growing enthusiasm for spas. Droitwich, the first traditional British spa to reopen, sits above an underground lake as saline as the Dead Sea, and has a clinic and a pool. Bath is due to reopen in 2002. Until then, if you want to visit a true spa, you need to go abroad.

**G**  Go to a spa, well-wishers suggested. But spas, or at least the health farms I've visited, are good fun for losing a few pounds, but as a way to tackle recurring bronchitis, it seemed an expensive, time-consuming long shot.

**H**  It depends on the importance ascribed to the water itself. Alice Kavounas says the composition of a mineral water is not what makes a spa effective. 'There is nothing special, for example, about the water at Lourdes,' she says. 'Any good water should contain a good deal of magnesium and calcium and very little nitrates. It's other factors that make the difference.'

## Part I

For questions 1–18, read the texts and decide which answer (**A**, **B**, **C** or **D**) best fits each gap.

---

### FAREWELL TO POSTMAN PAT

Postmen were once the most popular of public servants. Children collected stamps, young lovers eagerly (1) .............. news of each other, and even the sight of the postman being (2) .............. down the garden path by a fierce dog (3) .............. sympathy as well as amusement.

All that has changed. The Post Office, renamed Consignia in the (4) .............. hope that changing its name will solve its problems, is not doing its job. Less than 70% of first-class mail is (5) .............. the next day. Management now propose to (6) .............. the second post of the day, arguing that busy people do not need it. But busy people these days use fax and e-mail instead. It is the old who will miss the second delivery, just as they miss the friendly face of Postman Pat!

---

| 1 | **A** | waited | **B** | awaited | **C** | hoped | **D** | longed |
|---|---|---|---|---|---|---|---|---|
| 2 | **A** | tracked | **B** | persecuted | **C** | hunted | **D** | chased |
| 3 | **A** | aroused | **B** | raised | **C** | stirred | **D** | arose |
| 4 | **A** | poor | **B** | wrong | **C** | blind | **D** | vain |
| 5 | **A** | delivered | **B** | supplied | **C** | served | **D** | provided |
| 6 | **A** | knock out | **B** | rub out | **C** | do away with | **D** | make away with |

---

### ENOUGH SMALL CHANGE?

There were two main problems attending the (7) .............. of the euro in 2002. One was to decide how many coins would be needed. The other was concerned with distribution. While the new notes posed a much greater security (8) .............. and various features had to be (9) .............. into the design to prevent forgery, providing the right amount of hard (10) .............. was a greater worry.

The distribution problem (11) .............. from the fact that people would obtain notes from banks but coins would usually be handed over as change by retailers. Apart from that, no one had any idea how many coins were in (12) .............. because of the number lying around people's homes that suddenly needed to be exchanged.

---

| 7 | **A** | injection | **B** | insertion | **C** | innovation | **D** | introduction |
|---|---|---|---|---|---|---|---|---|
| 8 | **A** | risk | **B** | danger | **C** | hazard | **D** | chance |
| 9 | **A** | included | **B** | incorporated | **C** | joined | **D** | united |
| 10 | **A** | cash | **B** | coin | **C** | money | **D** | metal |
| 11 | **A** | branched | **B** | departed | **C** | led | **D** | stemmed |
| 12 | **A** | dissemination | **B** | circulation | **C** | publication | **D** | communication |

## HEALTH TAX

Everyone agrees that the National Health Service is (13) .............. short of funds but when the former minister, Peter Mandelson, proposed a health tax to meet the cost, the Chancellor, Mr Brown, would have (14) .............. of it.

Mr Mandelson is one of the Chancellor's (15) .............. aversions, but Mr Brown had more (16) .............. reasons for his refusal. The general public would not (17) .............. extra money to the health service (18) .............. it could see a link between what was paid and how it was spent. But the Treasury's view is that it must decide where the money goes, on the grounds that 'Mother knows best'

| 13 | A | desperately | B | hopelessly | C | greatly | D | largely |
|----|---|-------------|---|------------|---|---------|---|---------|
| 14 | A | none | B | nothing | C | no business | D | no interest |
| 15 | A | favourite | B | chosen | C | pet | D | preferred |
| 16 | A | prevailing | B | compelling | C | forceful | D | commanding |
| 17 | A | dislike | B | discuss | C | disagree | D | begrudge |
| 18 | A | so that | B | so far as | C | so long as | D | so much as |

### Tip

*You have one hour 30 minutes to complete the whole test. Do not spend too long on any one part, and remember that questions **1-18** are worth one mark, questions **19-40** are worth two!*

## Part 2

You are going to read four extracts on different topics. For questions **19–26**, choose the answer (**A, B, C** or **D**) which you think fits best according to the text.

---

### MAKING A START AS AN ART BUYER

Don't allow yourself to be carried away by current trends. Today's bargain may be tomorrow's flop. You can expect a certain amount of wear and tear on any object but you should always take a close look before bidding for anything.

A well made object is much more likely to appreciate in future than an expensive piece signed by a famous name. But signed prints by established names keep their value better than original works by unknowns.

It is helpful to have a second opinion, but your partner's tastes may not be the same as yours. Instinct is better than compromise. And what looks good in a dealer's shop may not be as attractive on your wall when you have had time to get used to it, and then you'll have to live with it.

---

**19**   What is the most reliable guide to an increase in value if you are buying as an investment?

   **A**   quality of workmanship

   **B**   the name of the artist

   **C**   prints rather than other works of art

   **D**   a bargain because the artist is unknown

**20**   What is the best way to go about buying a work of art from a dealer for the house you share with someone else?

   **A**   Go along with your partner and choose it together.

   **B**   Go alone but don't buy it until your partner has seen it.

   **C**   Buy something you feel sure your partner will like and take it home,

   **D**   Arrange with the dealer to take it home on approval to see how it looks.

**DON'T LET THE BANKS TAKE YOU FOR A RIDE!**

Banks and building societies employ a range of tactics to prevent savers from getting a good return.

A popular ploy is to launch an account that pays a high rate of interest, persuade you to invest in it, and then reduce the rate sharply after only a few months or weeks. Banks are obliged to write to customers and inform them of changes in the rates but most people do not read the letters, thinking they are junk mail, and the banks get away with it.

Banks may encourage people to invest by pointing out that the rate on their existing account is to be cut but they can switch to the new one, which offers a more attractive deal. But once enough money has been generated by these means, the banks slash the rates, relying on customers being too lazy to check what is going on.

The moral of the story is clear. Don't just read the small print in the first instance. Keep your eye on what is happening to your account at all times.

21    How do banks succeed by the technique outlined in the second paragraph?
   **A**   by not paying the rates of interest they have promised
   **B**   by cutting the rate almost immediately
   **C**   by neglecting to inform their customers
   **D**   by their customers not paying enough attention

22    In what way does the technique in the third paragraph differ from it?
   **A**   It is used on customers who already have a bank account.
   **B**   The bank puts pressure on customers, obliging them to change accounts.
   **C**   The bank waits until it has collected enough money before cutting rates.
   **D**   Customers are no longer able to check what is happening.

---

**PACKAGE HOLIDAYS HALVED IN PRICE**

As the holiday season nears its close, a package holiday war is due to start, with discounts of up to 50% for next year. Initially tour operators declared that they would cut capacity, not prices, but in the light of poor advance bookings over the past three months, they have been obliged to change their tune. While the response for Christmas and New Year holiday breaks has been in line with previous years, bookings for next summer are only half what they were at this time twelve months ago.

Operators emphasise that capacity has been reduced by about 15%, so that it is unrealistic to suggest that the industry is showing signs of panic and that they will be selling at any price. But there are still 10 million holidays to be sold and that means there will be aggressive discounting as the operators compete for custom. Customers on the look out for economical offers should have plenty to choose from.

---

**23** What is the reporter saying about tour operators in the first paragraph?

**A** Operators are competing strongly because of reduced capacity.

**B** Below average bookings for end-of-the-year holidays have caused them to change their plans.

**C** Customers' caution with regard to holidays next summer has caused them to reduce prices.

**D** Tour operators expected bookings to be double what they have been.

**24** What conclusion does the reporter reach in the second paragraph?

**A** The reduction in capacity will enable tour operators to survive.

**B** Tour operators will be driven to extreme lengths to sell holidays.

**C** Tour operators who lose the price war are likely to go out of business.

**D** Despite the reduction in capacity, many bargains should be available.

## IS MY MOBILE PHONE SAFE?

At a time when the world seems suddenly to have become full of people apparently jabbering away to themselves (once taken as a prime indication of lunacy) and shares in the mobile phone industry have rocketed up and then down on the stock exchange, it was perhaps inevitable that mobile phones would be the focus of the health scare of the year. Everyone knows that they emit radiation, and radiation kills, doesn't it? So all those who seem to spend hours with them clamped to their ears – while driving, riding bicycles or simply pacing up and down at airports – had better watch out, hadn't they?

The scientific answer, which also applies to television masts, PCs, microwave ovens and far more obviously lethal pieces of equipment comes in three forms – 'yes', 'no' and 'well, maybe.' Well-qualified scientists conducting impressive experiments not only disagree but when the discussion becomes really heated, do so violently. Those who try to calm things down are likely to be denounced as Government agents who owe their jobs to keeping things quiet. Those who try to stir things up are called mischief-makers or mad or are believed to be out for a large research grant to keep themselves in business. Responsible public bodies demonstrate their impartiality by publishing the conflicting reports and resolutely sitting on the fence.

25    What is the point that the writer is making in the first paragraph?
    A    People who make constant use of mobile phones look crazy.
    B    The health scare has had serious effects for the makers of mobile phones.
    C    It is not surprising that people relate mobile phones to health risks.
    D    Using mobile phones constantly is bound to affect people's hearing.

26    What does the writer suggest is the true official response to the questions raised?
    A    We think the risks have been exaggerated.
    B    We think a public warning ought to be issued.
    C    It is important to consider both points of view.
    D    We are not going to take sides in case we are proved wrong.

## Part 3

This article consists of 15 paragraphs. Seven of them have been removed. Choose from the paragraphs **A–H** the one that fits each gap (**27–33**). There is one extra paragraph that does not fit and which you do not need to use.

### IF YOU WANT TO KEEP THE TRAFFIC MOVING, BAN BUSES

The Mayor of London, in announcing his grand new traffic congestion scheme, claims that he has finished his long consultation with Londoners. Not so. No one has consulted me, despite the fact that I have been driving around central and greater London and using public transport almost all my adult life, and could be said to know something about it. I am even beginning to find that I know parts of London better than some taxi drivers.

| 27 |

By far the major cause of congestion, pollution and road rage in the streets of London is not the cars, as Ken seems to think, but the buses. Belching out diesel, buses sit for unaccountably long periods, idling extravagantly and holding up the traffic.

| 28 |

Without the nonsense of buses, London traffic would bowl along quite nicely. Anyone vaguely inclined to accept the idea that we must put up with the obvious obstruction of buses for the greater public good will soon be disabused.

| 29 |

In one of them a couple of broken-spirited public transport users sat meekly, apparently unaware that they were alone and that there was no one to drive the bus. For 20 minutes they sat there humbly, and when I unhumbly hailed a taxi, they were sitting there still. No doubt they were waiting for Ken!

| 30 |

However, it is not simply that buses are hopeless, inexcusably unreliable and obstructive. They also seem to be getting more and more dangerous. I don't know how bus drivers are trained or recruited these days, but to see them lurch in and out of the bus lane without proper signalling, or heave vertiginously round narrow intersections of ancient streets, is to despair and to hold your children close.

| 31 |

Almost as bad are the delivery lorries and builders' vans. London's booming economy has hugely swelled their size and numbers, too. But London remains, especially in its side streets, an 18th and 19th century city, quite unable to take refrigerated pantechnicons or double-parked commercial vehicles servicing conspicuous consumption.

| 32 |

We know that modern education means that many millions are unable to use the telephone directory, but it seems that in the past five years monster lorry drivers have at last learnt how to consult the London street map, and now imagine they can negotiate tiny side roads and clever local routes. Meanwhile, greedy builders double- and treble-park their vans for hours.

| 33 |

So, before it is too late, here is my suggestion. We should dump the red buses and allow much smaller, privately run people-carriers instead. We must pour millions into the Underground. Until then, the Mayor must not force yet more people on to public transport. If he does, there will be riots and death from overcrowding, overheating and public panic.

*Article by Minette Marrin © Telegraph Group Limited*

**A**  Buses are quite useless to anyone who is obliged to stick to a timetable. Two weeks ago at Russell Square, I found three parked together, at the same stop with the same number, any one of which could have taken me close to my destination. All three were unmanned.

**B**  Buses are too big for these streets and these drivers. The same applies to the ghastly tourist coaches, which grow bigger and bigger every year. In dumping wretched trippers at their hotels, they clog up entire narrow streets for half hour at a time. They, too, are too big to be allowed.

**C**  So I propose to offer Red Ken* the benefit of my experience at this eleventh hour. It is not too late, even though he has already issued his ambitious plan, because it is almost entirely unworkable, and he will have to change it.

**D**  In the meantime, all large coaches, all outsize lorries and vans, and all day-time deliveries should be excluded from London. Oh, and no cyclists. They are the most irresponsible, lawless and dangerous of the lot.

**E**  I sit amazed as these vast monsters ease themselves, bleeping, into Dickensian alleys. It is insanity. Quiet two-way streets, just passable for two modest vehicles abreast, are now clogged for hours on end while immense lorries blunder and bully their way through, bringing local – and 'community' – life to a standstill.

**F**  Meanwhile these useless, unused buses were obstructing a large square footage of public highway. Perhaps it is a sophisticated form of calming the traffic, like the mysterious road works everywhere, which are quite clearly unnecessary. I say nothing of the folly of the bus lane, a constant nightmare for cars and cyclists as they have to swerve suicidally in and out of them, if ever they are to turn.

**G**  It is daft that huge vehicles like this should be allowed to obstruct large parts of the public thoroughfare at regular intervals, while people must individually pay the driver before they can get on. At every stop, the entire nation is held up while people struggle for the right coins or the right exemption card.

**H**  And what is Red Ken's solution to all this? Not to keep out the real culprits, but to exclude the cars. And without a remotely usable public transport system in place instead. It is mad. Cars are not the problem; dependence on cars is a symptom of the problem.

* *Red Ken: the nickname of Ken Livingstone, the left-wing mayor of London*

## Part 4

You are going to read an article about holidays. For questions **34–40**, choose the answer (**A**, **B**, **C** or **D**) which you think fits best according to the text.

### WISH I WAS ALWAYS HERE

I am always amazed by the number of people who actively dislike taking holidays. At this time of year, you run into them all over the place, grumbling about their impending vacations, full of dark foreboding about what will surely go wrong.

For the fun-shy, this has been a vintage summer, with their gloomiest predictions fulfilled at every turn. Shark attacks off the Florida coast, travellers disappearing in the outback of Australia, brush fires sweeping across the Costa Brava and the south of France.

If these people are not fleeced by hawkers, then their blood will clot with deep vein thrombosis on the flight home. They will be struck down by heatstroke, be diddled on the currency by unscrupulous foreign money changers, delayed for days on end in the dreaded north terminal at Gatwick.

Warily, miserably, they are dragged kicking and screaming from their offices, convinced that no good can come of it, and that they will find the whole business more stressful than normal work. Incapable of enjoying holidays when they do take them, at a permanent loose end around the pool, they moan about settling back into their routines and punch furiously at the buttons of their mobile phones. And they feel guilty about taking time off at all, fearful of office coups when they're not there to watch their backs.

To all these people, I have only one thing to say: how very sad you are.

I love every aspect of being on holiday: the first rush of warm air against your face when you land at an exotic airport, wearing swimming trunks and dark glasses at breakfast time, spending foreign money in shops so you never quite know what anything costs, and having nothing special to do.

I vastly prefer my holiday wardrobe of coloured linen shirts to the suits I feel I have to wear to work. Although normally prone to slight workaholic tendencies, on holiday I am perfectly content to bask on a lilo for several hours at a time.

Working as I do for an American-owned media company, holiday dates tend to be prescribed. In England, executives take staggered holidays throughout the year, a fortnight here and a week there, but Americans bunk off en masse in August and over Christmastide and New Year. Increasingly, I follow this pattern myself because the normal stream of faxes and e-mails dries to a trickle, and I can disengage more completely from office events.

Over time, I have perfected the routine for my ideal holiday day. The morning is spent sitting on a deckchair overlooking a twinkling blue sea. From time to time, drinks are delivered by smiling waiters. The weather should be blazing hot and the land brown and arid, without much to look at, which makes it more restful. If I can't have sea, I will settle for long views of hills. It doesn't matter where these are. What matters is the sun and the view.

At lunchtime, I like to eat outside under an umbrella, never in a stuffy hotel dining room. In the afternoon, I go for a very long hot walk or do some water-skiing. Then a hot bath, in which my sunburnt skin should hurt as I ease it into the scalding water. An early dinner, lots of jokes with the children, some cheerful gossip with friends, bed by 11.

The most difficult thing, I find, is achieving the right balance between cosmic calm and social stimulation. Before going on holiday, I always imagine I want to see nobody at all, just the family, to aid the relaxation process. The last thing we need, I hear myself saying, is a house full of friends demanding to be entertained from morning till night. The whole point of a holiday is getting away from all that. After 10 days on our own, however, we sometimes become slightly stale and long for friendly faces.

People who fuss about holiday illnesses astonish me. I am never ill on holiday and I never take precautions. I never wear sun cream or have injections or immunisations, even for India or Africa. I cling to the illogical belief that nothing can possibly go wrong. Once, in Belize, we went for a two-hour stroll along the river bank in the jungle. I was barefoot. Afterwards, the appalled hotel manager told us the undergrowth was teeming with fer-de-lance, Central America's most poisonous small snake. Its bite is fatal in seven seconds.

I am suspicious of colleagues who don't take up their full holiday allocations. It indicates limited intellectual curiosity, bad planning and a deficient capacity for pleasure, which could undermine their performance in their jobs. People who resolutely refuse to take holidays, claiming pressure of work, are invariably petty, insecure, disorganised and heading for a breakdown.

The proper length for a holiday is three weeks, which gives you a whole week at the beginning when time appears to stretch out before you into infinity, and you can hardly see the end. A fortnight is never quite long enough, since you hit the half-way mark after only seven days. The final week is, for me, always a bit of a washout, since I start to become twitchy again about work, and can't resist ringing the office every day to pick up the threads.

I find that the afterglow of a good holiday can last from four to five months before the benefit begins to wear off. And then it is time to start anticipating the next one. Even the prospect of sunlight and beach life, ages ahead, is enough to sustain me through months of remorseless work.

*Article by Nicholas Coleridge, published in The Telegraph.*
*© Nicholas Coleridge*

**34**   What is the subject of the first three paragraphs of the writer's article?

   **A**   The fears of people who don't look forward to going on holiday.

   **B**   The dangers awaiting those going abroad on holiday.

   **C**   The probability of being cheated by foreigners when abroad.

   **D**   The exceptionally bad sequence of events for holidaymakers this year.

**35**   Which of these adjectives best summarises the writer's opinion of those who do not enjoy holidays?

   **A**   stressed

   **B**   bad-tempered

   **C**   paranoiac

   **D**   pathetic

**36**   Which element appears to be indispensable for the writer's enjoyment of a holiday?

   **A**   sunshine

   **B**   idleness

   **C**   changes of clothes

   **D**   the sea

**37**   Why is it an advantage for him to work for an American company?

   **A**   He can follow the pattern laid down by the President.

   **B**   He can choose when he goes on holiday.

   **C**   Everyone else is on holiday at the same time.

   **D**   He knows his privacy will be respected while he is away.

**38**   Which of these does he enjoy most on holiday?

   **A**   rest

   **B**   good company

   **C**   interesting places to visit

   **D**   night life

**39**   To what does he attribute his good health on holiday?

   **A**   advice taken before going on holiday

   **B**   advice taken from local people

   **C**   preparation for everything that could go wrong

   **D**   sheer luck

**40**   In his opinion, people who take few holidays

   **A**   are more hard-working.

   **B**   are better workers.

   **C**   are not as efficient.

   **D**   resent colleagues who take their full allowance.

## Part I

For questions **1–18**, read the texts and decide which answer (**A, B, C** or **D**) best fits each gap.

### MONSTER WAVES

German scientists claim to have explained the mystery behind monster waves more than 40 m high, thought to have sunk more than 200 large ships without (1) ............... in the past 20 years. Often (2) ............... as absurd, such waves have provided the raw material for (3) ............... novels and films. Yet until now no one knew what formed such gigantic seas, capable of breaking a ship in half and sending it to the (4) ............... in seconds. By simulating them in a tank, scientists have shown that they occur when slow-moving waves are (5) ............... by a succession of faster waves in a storm. The research will help naval architects to construct safer vessels, with a rounded bridge. Most ships at present are not built along these (6) ............... .

| | | | | | | | |
|---|---|---|---|---|---|---|---|
| **1** | **A** sign | **B** mark | **C** trace | **D** track |
| **2** | **A** dismissed | **B** overlooked | **C** neglected | **D** underestimated |
| **3** | **A** uncountable | **B** interminable | **C** incalculable | **D** countless |
| **4** | **A** bottom | **B** deck | **C** floor | **D** depth |
| **5** | **A** overcome | **B** overflowed | **C** overruled | **D** overtaken |
| **6** | **A** designs | **B** lines | **C** styles | **D** types |

### A GHOST IN HANDEL'S HOUSE

The house where the composer Handel lived in London is to be exorcised after two people claim to have seen a ghost there. The Handel Trust thought the news might (7) ............... visitors ............... so it decided that the wisest (8) ............... to follow was to (9) ............... of it. The ghost seemed to be that of a woman, and staff working in the house reported a (10) ............... smell of perfume. No one knows who the ghost might be but, as Handel never married, the two most promising (11) ............... were his only frequent women visitors, rival sopranos seeking to (12) ............... themselves with him and land star parts in his operas.

| | | | | | | | |
|---|---|---|---|---|---|---|---|
| **7** | **A** keep ... off | **B** drive ... away | **C** hold ... back | **D** turn ... out |
| **8** | **A** course | **B** action | **C** way | **D** method |
| **9** | **A** dispense | **B** get rid | **C** let go | **D** give up |
| **10** | **A** lingering | **B** staying | **C** remaining | **D** residing |
| **11** | **A** entries | **B** challengers | **C** candidates | **D** competitors |
| **12** | **A** insinuate | **B** favour | **C** influence | **D** ingratiate |

## CAPTAIN MORGAN'S TREASURE

A German treasure hunter claims to have found the ship of the 17th-century Welsh buccaneer, Henry Morgan, who made his (13) .............. robbing merchant ships in the Caribbean. The ship sank off the coast of Haiti, but the exact position of the wreck is being kept secret to (14) .............. other fortune hunters.

A buccaneer is a pirate who (15) .............. from attacking ships of his own country. The English government supported Morgan until he attacked Panama, (16) .............. that a peace treaty with Spain had just been signed. Luckily for him, relations with Spain (17) .............. before he went on trial. Instead of being (18) .............. to death, he was knighted, made Deputy Governor of Jamaica, and died in his bed a wealthy man!

| 13 | **A** business | **B** affair | **C** fortune | **D** occupation |
|----|----|----|----|----|
| 14 | **A** discourage | **B** disgust | **C** displease | **D** distract |
| 15 | **A** avoids | **B** evades | **C** refrains | **D** withdraws |
| 16 | **A** ignorant | **B** unconscious | **C** unknown | **D** unaware |
| 17 | **A** declined | **B** decayed | **C** destroyed | **D** deteriorated |
| 18 | **A** executed | **B** put | **C** taken | **D** sent |

## *Vocabulary Development*

Complete the sentences below with a word or phrase taken from the choices for the questions you have answered. The sentences are printed in the same order as the questions. Note the difference between the correct answer below and a phrase of similar meaning in the passages above.

1   Many believe the experts have ................................. the number of ships sunk by huge waves and the true figure is far more than 200.

2   Nouns like *wealth* that have no plural are called ................................. nouns.

3   The house was flooded when the river nearby ................................. its banks.

4   The trustees thought exorcising the ghost was the wisest course of ................................. .

5   The two sopranos were ................................. , trying to get the same roles.

6   Each of them called on him, hoping to ................................. him in her favour.

7   They tried to ................................. other fortune hunters from the search by issuing false information.

8   The film *Captain Blood*, starring Errol Flynn, was about a buccaneer like Morgan who fights bravely, ................................. the enemy ships, and is rewarded.

9   Spanish influence on the American continent ................................. during the 17th century.

10   Most pirates were ................................. when they were caught, unlike Morgan.

*Part 2*

These two texts relate to things that people have always regarded as mysterious. For questions **19–22**, choose the answer (**A**, **B**, **C** or **D**) which you think fits best according to the text.

## NO MORE ROMANCE IN THE MOON?

Until the astronauts landed on its surface just over 30 years ago, the moon was still suffused with mystery, as it was for our ancestors. In the ancient world it was feared and worshipped and the poets of almost every nation have sung its praises, or, like Shakespeare's Juliet, bemoaned its inconstancy. Her conception of the moon was that of the popular imagination. The moon is feminine, unpredictable, an object that constantly appears to change its shape, the opposite of the sun. Yet at the same time, no doubt because of its faint but fascinating light, it has always combined romance with mystery, contrasted to the 'clear light of day'.

The moon landing changed all that. The trouble with the moon is that from a scientific point of view, it is rather dull. Once you take away the myths and the legends, the moon is just a lot of rocks and dust. Mars still retains our curiosity because there may have been some life there once. But three years after the excitement of the climax to the race to be the first to the moon, manned missions ceased and have not been resumed. And perhaps the moon seems less magical to us because only if we live far from cities in unpolluted air can we still walk through a wood illuminated solely by its light.

**19**   Juliet's idea of the moon was typical because she regarded it as

    **A**   frightening.

    **B**   holy.

    **C**   changeable.

    **D**   female, like herself.

**20**   Why, in the writer's opinion, do we no longer regard the moon as romantic?

    **A**   We lost interest when we saw that nothing has ever lived there.

    **B**   Nowadays people are more attracted to Mars.

    **C**   Exploration of the moon has ceased.

    **D**   Most of us are unable to experience its attraction.

### NESSIE STILL ALIVE AND SWIMMING?

Sightings at Loch Ness of Scotland's favourite monster, affectionately known as Nessie, are frequent enough for a prize of £1,000 to be offered annually to the photographer submitting the best picture. This is despite the suggestion made by the famous Italian seismologist, Dr Piccardi, that she is a product of underwater volcanic activity. Dr Piccardi argued that the only thing all the pictures have in common is a splash like that of an earth tremor.

Local geologists disagree, saying there have never been tremors in the area, and the winning pictures in the competition contradict the theory, too. One shows what looks like a neck, much larger than human, emerging from the water. The other shows a strange humped object about 8 m long half way across the lake at its deepest point (over 200 m). The judges ruled out any chance of a hoax at that distance from the shore, and said it could not be a boat, a wave, a shadow, or a reflection.

A fisherman took several photographs of something that rose 2 m out of the water, with a long black neck, like that of a conger eel. But these eels do not live in fresh water. Zoologists rejected the claim, saying it was probably the branch of a tree, but not long afterwards holidaymakers found two dead conger eels on the shore. How did they get there? They could have been dumped from a fishing boat or might just possibly prove the argument, put forward long ago, that there is an underwater link between the lake and the ocean. Then again, maybe this was just someone's idea of a practical joke.

**21**  Why is Dr Piccardi's theory accounting for Nessie unlikely to be correct?

  **A**  There is no longer any volcanic activity in the lake.

  **B**  The pictures taken of the monster are so different.

  **C**  The pictures taken this year disprove it.

  **D**  The pictures taken are undoubtedly genuine.

**22**  Which of these explanations for the fisherman's photographs would explain the mystery?

  **A**  They were of a large species of eel that lives in the lake.

  **B**  They were of a dead eel that had been thrown overboard.

  **C**  They were of two eels later found beside the lake.

  **D**  They were of an eel that had found a way in from the sea.

---

**Active Vocabulary List**

These are some words and phrases closely connected with the subject of mysteries. If you are not sure of the meaning of any words or phrases, look them up in your dictionary.

| | |
|---|---|
| mystery, supernatural, paranormal | alien, UFO |
| ghost, spirit, poltergeist, haunted | psychic phenomena, telepathy |
| clairvoyant, fortune teller | spiritualist, medium, séance |
| omen, premonition, prediction | superstition, evil eye, witch |

## Part 3 (Ordering paragraphs)

This article consists of 15 paragraphs. Seven of them have been removed. Choose from the paragraphs **A-H** the one that fits each gap (**23-29**). There is one extra paragraph that does not fit and which you do not need to use.

### SUSPECT HELD OVER MURDER OF FOSSEY

The mystery surrounding the brutal murder of Dian Fossey, the world-renowned American naturalist who worked with rare and endangered mountain gorillas, may finally be solved more than 15 years after she was hacked to death in the African rainforest. The FBI will apply this week to interview a man the Belgian police have detained in connection with the 1994 Rwandan genocide. He is also suspected of being the mastermind behind Fossey's death.

**23**

An intruder had broken into her two-room corrugated shack and her skull had been split open by blows with a machete. Her last diary entry read: 'When you realise the value of all life, you dwell less on what is past and concentrate on the preservation of the future.' The Rwandan authorities quickly arrested an employee of the camp, who apparently committed suicide in prison.

**24**

Those who knew him found the case against him preposterous. They were convinced the Rwandans were looking for a western scapegoat for a murder they had themselves ordered because Fossey had become an irritation to them. The investigation had been conducted amateurishly and diplomats believed the Rwandan tracker said to have hanged himself in his cell had been killed to keep him from talking.

**25**

The finger of suspicion among diplomats pointed almost from the start at Protais Zigiranyirazo. But because his sister was married to the then president, Juvenal Habyiramana, he was virtually above the law.

**26**

For years the FBI found this prime suspect untouchable. All this changed last Thursday when Zigiranyirazo was arrested in Belgium. He will appear in a Brussels court tomorrow on an extradition warrant from the international war crimes tribunal for Rwanda, which was set up to punish the perpetrators of the genocide.

**27**

At the time of Fossey's death, he was the powerful governor of the province in north-west Rwanda where she had been working for 18 years to study and save the mountain gorillas. He was a member of the Akazu, the president's inner circle. When the president was assassinated in 1994 it was the Akazu that unleashed the slaughter. In three months, about 800,000 people, mostly from the Tutsi minority of Rwanda, were murdered on its orders.

**28**

The antagonism between Fossey and Zigiranyirazo had started several years earlier, some time before her death. She had made many enemies in Rwanda, particularly after poachers killed Digit, her favourite gorilla. Her focus switched almost entirely from conservation and research to the ever more critical battle against poaching.

**29**

In early 1985 she interrogated one of the country's biggest poachers and sent reports to Zigiranyirazo demanding action against dozens of others. She was killed when diplomats believe she was about to pass on the information outside the country. This would have caused Zigiranyirazo and the Habyiramana regime serious embarrassment.

*Article by Jon Swain, © The Sunday Times*

**A**  Fossey's work in Rwanda was portrayed by Sigourney Weaver in the film *Gorillas in the Mist* while in the country today Zigiranyirazo is near the top of the wanted list for the actions of his death squads during the genocide.

**B**  The most obvious suspects were local poachers and smugglers but the plot to kill Fossey was almost certainly planned at a high level, as diplomats indicated at the time. She had campaigned relentlessly to halt poaching and gold smuggling, and opposed opening up the gorillas' sanctuaries to tourism, fearing this would destroy their habitat.

**C**  Travelling on false French identity papers, he had arrived in Belgium from Kenya, where he had been living for several years. When the Belgian authorities detained him as an illegal immigrant he applied for political asylum. But once his real identity became clear, they notified the chief prosecutor at the war crimes tribunal, and the FBI.

**D**  Her body was discovered on December 27, 1985, at Karisoke, her remote research station 3,000 m up in the mist-shrouded Virunga mountains along Rwanda's border with Uganda and the Congo.

**E**  Zigiranyirazo was allegedly involved in illegal trading in endangered species and gold smuggling out of the Congo. Diplomats believe Fossey was about to expose him.

**F**  Her hatred for the poachers who sold gorillas' hands and feet as souvenirs knew no bounds. By 1981, six of the eighty gorillas she had been studying had been killed and the skeletal remains of 60 others led her to suspect that systematic poaching was organised from the top of the local administration, led by Zigiranyirazo.

**G**  When the extremists of the Hutu majority were defeated in the autumn of that year, however, Rwanda came under Tutsi rule. Zigiranyirazo fled first to France, where his sister Agathe still lives, and then to Kenya, where, in common with other prime genocide suspects, he enjoyed high-level political protection.

**H**  Some months later Wayne McGuire, Fossey's American research assistant, was tipped off by the US embassy that he was about to be arrested. He fled to America and was sentenced to death in his absence by the Rwandans for her murder.

*Part 1*

For questions 1–18, read the texts and decide which answer (**A, B, C** or **D**) best fits each gap.

## KEEP OFF THE GRASS!

Grass is a unique plant because its elaborate root system has power to (1) .............. the soil with compounds known as humus. The method that takes full (2) .............. of this is mixed arable and livestock farming, using crop rotation. Cattle graze on the pastures, which after four years are ploughed up and (3) .............. with crops, while the land exhausted by food production is given a rest.

This method is now virtually (4) .............. in Britain since the policy of paying higher subsidies to single-crop farms encouraged farmers to put their (5) .............. in chemical fertilisers instead of rotation. This damages the soil and destroys the wildlife. In the view of ecologists, the policy really subsidises the chemical industry, (6) .............. waste to the countryside in the process.

| 1 | **A** enhance | **B** enrich | **C** revalue | **D** pick up |
|---|---|---|---|---|
| 2 | **A** advantage | **B** profit | **C** benefit | **D** gain |
| 3 | **A** scattered | **B** sprinkled | **C** coated | **D** sown |
| 4 | **A** antiquated | **B** extinct | **C** obsolete | **D** vanished |
| 5 | **A** preference | **B** reliance | **C** trust | **D** belief |
| 6 | **A** making | **B** laying | **C** running | **D** leaving |

## DEFORESTATION

Deforestation is generally thought of as a recent phenomenon. But it has a long history, (7) .............. back to the first use of fire by human beings. (8) .............. down trees is part of the eternal (9) .............. for shelter and warmth. All that has happened since 1950 is that the process has been (10) .............. by modern tools and more sensitive environments have been damaged, perhaps permanently.

Until metal tools (11) .............. stone axes about 3,500 years ago, clearing the forest to grow crops was an arduous task. But this does not mean that it did not take place. (12) .............. , the evidence goes to show that farmers in Europe in the Neolithic period behaved very much like the pioneers in the United States in the last century.

| 7 | **A** branching | **B** bridging | **C** carrying | **D** stretching |
|---|---|---|---|---|
| 8 | **A** Chopping | **B** Chipping | **C** Carving | **D** Clipping |
| 9 | **A** pursuit | **B** persecution | **C** chase | **D** quest |
| 10 | **A** accelerated | **B** speeded | **C** hurried | **D** raced |
| 11 | **A** substituted | **B** overtook | **C** replaced | **D** exchanged |
| 12 | **A** On the other hand | **B** On the contrary | **C** In contrast | **D** In contradiction |

## JUST FOLLOW 'MOTHER'

A story just published concerns some rare birds, whooping cranes, that have forgotten how to migrate. The cranes are (13) .............. a training programme, aimed at reversing the decline in their numbers, which have (14) .............. sharply. They must fly 2,500 km across the USA but as they were (15) .............. in captivity, they do not know the (16) .............. . If the experiment is successful, they will follow a plane to Florida and return by themselves in the spring.

Before the chicks were even born, recordings of the aircraft's engine were played next to their shells so they would get (17) .............. to the noise. They cannot fly yet but hop behind a light moving slowly along the airstrip. In six months' time, it is hoped that the plane will (18) .............. and the birds will fly after it.

| | | | | | | | | |
|----|---|---------|---|-------------|---|-----------|---|-------------|
| 13 | A | enduring | B | encountering | C | undergoing | D | undertaking |
| 14 | A | fallen down | B | fallen off | C | fallen out | D | fallen short |
| 15 | A | bred | B | brought up | C | grown up | D | developed |
| 16 | A | course | B | road | C | direction | D | way |
| 17 | A | accustomed | B | familiar | C | tamed | D | experienced |
| 18 | A | rise off | B | raise up | C | lift up | D | take off |

## Vocabulary Development

Complete the sentences below with a word or phrase taken from the choices for the questions you have answered. The sentences are printed in the same order as the questions. Note the difference between the correct answer below and a phrase of similar meaning in the passages above.

1    The agents are sure to ................................... the house now the airport has been built.

2    I've ................................... a little pepper on the salad.

3    The mammoth, a giant elephant, has been ................................... for thousands of years.

4    The thief ran away with the policeman in hot ...................................

5    Modern tools ................................... up the process considerably.

6    The pioneers exterminated the bison that lived on the prairies, ................................... to the native Americans, who realised how useful they were.

7    The Operation Migration project is ................................... the cost of the training.

8    He was ................................... by an aunt after his parents' death.

9    By the time they were born, the birds were already ................................... with the noise of the engine.

10   It will be wonderful to see the plane ................................... the ground and birds take off after it.

## Part 2

These two texts relate to issues concerning the environment. For questions **19–22**, choose the answer (**A**, **B**, **C** or **D**) which you think fits best according to the text.

### ATTITUDES TO ENERGY SAVING

Although, according to a recent survey, 80% of adults in Britain are aware of such threats to the environment as global warming and the destruction of the ozone layer, 49% said they were not concerned, and 26% claimed there was no problem to be faced. In fact, it cannot be denied that the environment is affected by the way we live, and if we are to have hot water, heat and light at the flick of a switch, there is a price to be paid.

People were also asked if they could do more to save energy in their own homes. The majority did not waste energy unnecessarily but were not as careful as the organisers would have liked. Most of us do switch off the light when no one is in the room, switch off the heating when no one is at home, and save water by having a shower instead of a bath. Seventy per cent also claimed to take bottles, cans or paper to be recycled. But half of those interviewed left clothes to dry on radiators, absorbing heat, and left doors open, and quite a lot of people leave the television or their PC on standby when it is not in use.

After living in England for five years, I have returned to a warmer climate. In all but one respect I am once more a model consumer. But if I was not one when I lived there, I feel that there was some excuse. Though I worked with a PC every day, I always turned it off at night. But how do you aid the recycling process if the local council, unlike the one here, provide no containers? How do you get clothes dry in winter if it rains most of the time and you have no indoor facilities? And surely a house where the doors stay permanently shut is secretive, forbidding and unhealthy?

**19**  Which adjective best describes the attitude of almost half the population to global warming?

    **A**  ignorant

    **B**  indifferent

    **C**  careless

    **D**  defiant

**20**  Which is the one respect in which the writer is still not a model consumer?

    **A**  He does not make use of recycling facilities.

    **B**  He dries his clothes on the radiator.

    **C**  He leaves doors open.

    **D**  He leaves the PC on standby.

### FORECASTING THE WEATHER

The meteorologists on television when I lived in Britain always exuded an air of total conviction, despite such monumental bloomers as one of them remarking just before a hurricane struck the south of England in 1987 that people ringing up in alarm were talking nonsense. Here by the Mediterranean, the forecast on TV does not carry quite the same air of authority, even though the weather is in theory more predictable. This may be because the weather forecasters who whip through it at breakneck speed are more concerned about their hairdo than the charts.

Things are said to be getting better. While long-range forecasts of more than 10 days are still too unreliable to be offered to the general public, satellites are seeing through the clouds to read temperature, air movements and rainfall with unprecedented accuracy. The fly in the ointment appears to be what is aptly termed 'chaos theory'. Minor fluctuations in ocean temperatures can have huge consequences. That is why we see a mass rushing across the Atlantic but cannot be quite sure how soon it will reach us or how strong it will be, or whether it will change direction and make someone else's life miserable instead.

**21**   The most serious mistake reported in the first paragraph was due to the weather forecaster on TV

   **A**   being too self-important to listen.

   **B**   dismissing the evidence.

   **C**   reading the information too quickly.

   **D**   being too concerned about her appearance.

**22**   Why is it still impossible to make accurate long-term forecasts?

   **A**   Because the public cannot be trusted with the information.

   **B**   Because of disagreements between the scientists.

   **C**   Because the equipment is still inadequate.

   **D**   Because of small changes that affect weather elsewhere.

### Active Vocabulary List

These are some words and phrases closely connected with the subject of the environment. If you are not sure of the meaning of any words or phrases, look them up in your dictionary.

| | |
|---|---|
| acid rain, smog, clean air | traffic congestion, fumes |
| global warming, greenhouse effect | ozone layer, ultraviolet light |
| wildlife, endangered species, extinct | rainforest, woodland, wetlands |
| organic crops, pesticide | pollution, contamination, toxic waste |
| recycling, solar power, wind power | renewable energy, sustainable source |

## Part 3 (Multiple-choice comprehension)

Read this article about the state of the world's oceans. For questions **23–29**, choose the answer (**A**, **B**, **C** or **D**) which you think fits best according to the text.

### IN DEEP WATER

The oceans once teemed with 'fantastic abundances' of large fish, from sharks to cod. They held many billions of marine mammals and reptiles including whales, dolphins, sea cows and turtles. Oysters and other shellfish formed huge reefs that would have been a serious hazard to modern shipping.

The astonishing richness of marine life before mankind started to plunder the seas emerges in an international study published yesterday in the journal *Science.* The paper, by 19 of the world's leading marine biologists, is written in sober academic language but it paints a shocking picture of the destruction wrought by many centuries of global overfishing. In the context of such dramatic long-term changes, this week's heated discussions at the International Whaling Commission in London, affecting the fate of a few thousand whales a year at most, seem almost trivial. Whale populations may have recovered to some extent during the moratorium on commercial whaling in the past 15 years but they are at a fraction of their pre-industrial levels.

The scientists found that overfishing has been destroying ecosystems for many centuries. (They define overfishing as the excessive removal of any marine organism, not only true fish but also mammals, reptiles, invertebrates and plants.) They started out to study everything people had ever done to oceans historically and were astounded to discover that in each case they examined, overfishing was the primary driver of ecosystem collapse. Many ecological disasters previously blamed on pollution turn out to be due to overfishing.

The new study combines geological, archaeological, historical and ecological data, providing a long-term perspective missing from previous research into marine ecology. 'Even seemingly gloomy estimates of the global percentages of fish stocks that are overfished are almost certainly far too low,' it concludes.

Chesapeake Bay on the US east coast illustrates the issues in microcosm. The first European settlers found water so clear that a lost cannon could be seen on the sea bed 10m down. Grey whales, dolphins, and many other species were all abundant. Today they have either disappeared or are represented by a tiny remnant population that has no significant impact on the ecology. The waters of the Chesapeake are a cloudy soup of bacteria and algae, overloaded with nutrients and starved of oxygen.

The primary source of the problem is not agricultural pollution, as many environmentalists believe, but the destruction of the bay's gigantic oyster reefs after mechanical harvesting started in the 19th century. Oysters are extremely efficient at cleaning sea water by removing bacteria, algae and excessive nutrients. Once they had been removed, the quality of such an enclosed body of water was bound to deteriorate.

The story of the kelp (brown seaweed) forests of the northern Pacific is especially complicated. Before people arrived in the region, there was a balance between sea urchins grazing the kelp and sea otters eating the urchins. About 2,500 years ago, otter hunting by the native Aleuts started to remove most of these predators, enabling urchins to overgraze the kelp, a process that accelerated with the commercial hunting of otters for their fur in the 19th century. When the sea otter came under legal protection in the late 20th century, their numbers increased, sea urchins declined, and the kelp grew back. But this process has recently gone into reverse. Killer whales have started eating otters because seals and sea lions, their natural prey, are declining as the result of overfishing.

In the north Atlantic kelp forests of the Gulf of Maine, large fish such as cod were the main predators of sea urchins. Removal of most coastal cod through overfishing has increased the number of urchins and laid the foundations for Maine's growing lobster industry. Lobsters are thriving because cod and other predators are no longer around to eat their young. But the lobster boom may be unsustainable. In Maine there is a very unstable coastal ecosystem today, with changes occurring at the scale of years to decades, not centuries to millennia, as was formerly the case.

Although the conclusions of their study are so depressing, the researchers offer some hope. Few large sea animals have been completely wiped out and, where remnant populations survive, restoration is a possibility. An expanded global network of marine reserves, in which all fishing and extractive activities are banned, could provide the nucleus for recovery. Fishermen are often hostile to proposed reserves. They see them as taking away rather than contributing to their livelihoods. Their negative perception is reinforced by long experience with a growing body of regulations that have failed to halt fishery declines. But the scientific evidence shows that protection from fishing quickly raises the size and population density of marine animals, helping to stock commercial fisheries outside the reserves.

The ultimate message of the study must be encouraging. The oceans once supported a richness of life beyond the imagination of most people alive today, and with proper management the bounty could return.

*Article by Clive Cookson © Financial Times Ltd*

23    Which of the terms used by the writer in the second paragraph implies the strongest moral criticism of human activity in the oceans?

  **A**  plunder

  **B**  shocking

  **C**  destruction

  **D**  trivial

24    In view of the study in *Science,* the arguments at the meeting in London appear

  **A**  excitable.

  **B**  absurd.

  **C**  relatively unimportant.

  **D**  totally irrelevant.

25    What does the study say about the effects of overfishing?

  **A**  They had never previously been investigated.

  **B**  They are probably much worse than indicated.

  **C**  The human contribution to them has been exaggerated.

  **D**  The opinions of most environmentalists have been proved correct.

26    Why is the water of Chesapeake Bay no longer clear?

  **A**  All the species once found there have gone.

  **B**  Farming on the shore has affected it.

  **C**  Fishermen killed the species that kept it clean.

  **D**  Bacteria were introduced into it.

27    What activity caused an increase in the growth of kelp in the north Pacific?

  **A**  Men began to hunt sea otters.

  **B**  Men were forbidden to hunt sea otters.

  **C**  Killer whales changed their diet.

  **D**  Men overfished seals and sea lions.

28    What produced a more satisfactory situation in Maine?

  **A**  The kelp forests are growing faster.

  **B**  There are more sea urchins.

  **C**  Cod numbers have declined.

  **D**  The changes in the pattern have taken place more quickly.

29    Which of these adjectives best describes the fishermen's response to marine reserves?

  **A**  selfish

  **B**  unjustified

  **C**  ignorant

  **D**  short-sighted

## Part 1

For questions 1–18, read the texts and decide which answer (**A**, **B**, **C** or **D**) best fits each gap.

### SUMMER COURSES FOR CHILDREN

Children may not want to go out to play in winter but the fine weather in summer ought to coax them out of doors. The trouble is that that's just when schools (1) .............. for the holidays and team games become more difficult to organise.

Parents are constantly being warned that the younger (2) .............. is unhealthily obese, so this is the time to (3) .............. steps to counteract it. The first (4) .............. of call should be the local authority. Provision of activities varies according to the number of volunteers available to (5) .............. them, but the quality is guaranteed. The only problem is that children can only participate where you pay taxes, which is a little unfair on those living in areas with poor (6) .............. .

| | | | | | | | | |
|---|---|---|---|---|---|---|---|---|
| 1 | **A** | lock up | **B** | lock out | **C** | break up | **D** | break out |
| 2 | **A** | breed | **B** | generation | **C** | race | **D** | stock |
| 3 | **A** | make | **B** | do | **C** | bring | **D** | take |
| 4 | **A** | place | **B** | halt | **C** | harbour | **D** | port |
| 5 | **A** | supervise | **B** | govern | **C** | dictate | **D** | dominate |
| 6 | **A** | assets | **B** | means | **C** | resources | **D** | wealth |

### FOOTBALLERS' WIVES

When ITV launched a new series with this title, the content was sadly predictable. It was full of beautiful blondes living in the lap of (7) .............. and (8) .............. all their energies to buying clothes and planning their getaway with the latest handsome import from abroad, with or without a transfer (9) .............. .

In real life, these women seldom (10) .............. to the standard characters in a soap opera. Like their husbands, they usually come from humble family (11) .............. , and are as inarticulate. They are not welcome at the club in case they cause trouble among the players. Their husbands' shocking behaviour on and off the field is faithfully reported in the popular newspapers. In short, their lives are not really much (12) .............. .

| | | | | | | | | |
|---|---|---|---|---|---|---|---|---|
| 7 | **A** | prosperity | **B** | luxury | **C** | wealth | **D** | comfort |
| 8 | **A** | devoting | **B** | lending | **C** | disposing | **D** | spending |
| 9 | **A** | charge | **B** | price | **C** | fee | **D** | bill |
| 10 | **A** | resemble | **B** | conform | **C** | comply | **D** | imitate |
| 11 | **A** | backgrounds | **B** | circumstances | **C** | atmospheres | **D** | settings |
| 12 | **A** | enjoyment | **B** | amusement | **C** | pleasure | **D** | fun |

### THE END OF THE ROAD FOR PISTOL PETE?

Pete Sampras is acknowledged to be the best tennis player of his generation and perhaps the best grass court player of all time. He doesn't seem ready to (13) .............. , though he is asked at every press conference if he is willing to call it (14) .............. . But every time the question (15) .............. up, he patiently explains that he is still hungry for success.

The title that still (16) .............. him is the major championship on slow clay in Paris. I am a great admirer of Sampras but I'm afraid his hopes will always be (17) .............. . His wonderful serve-and-volley game is perfectly attuned to grass, but it takes superhuman skill to attack like that on clay and (18) .............. with it.

| 13 | **A** resign | **B** dismiss | **C** abandon | **D** retire |
|----|----|----|----|----|
| 14 | **A** a day | **B** an end | **C** a stop | **D** a term |
| 15 | **A** shows | **B** crops | **C** blows | **D** follows |
| 16 | **A** avoids | **B** resists | **C** eludes | **D** dodges |
| 17 | **A** disillusioned | **B** disappointed | **C** dissatisfied | **D** disrupted |
| 18 | **A** get away | **B** get off | **C** get on | **D** get over |

## Vocabulary Development

Complete the sentences below with a word or phrase taken from the choices for the questions you have answered. The sentences are printed in the same order as the questions. Note the difference between the correct answer below and a phrase of similar meaning in the passages above.

1   They need tighter security in the prison if they don't want the prisoners to ................................. .

2   Parents should ................................. an effort to counteract obesity in their children.

3   Playing fields that cannot be sold are known technically as fixed ................................. .

4   'I'll take this and that, and that and this,' she said. 'Send the ................................. to my husband at the club.'

5   These women are very different from TV characters in real life and seldom ................................. them.

6   'I've got a personality of my own,' she said. 'I don't need to ................................. those characters on TV.'

7   Like her husband, she grew up in humble ................................. .

8   Government ministers never admit their mistakes if it means they would have to ................................. .

9   When he first entered for the championship, he had high hopes of winning, but he's lost so many times that by now he's completely ................................. .

10   I wish they'd stop arguing and ................................. with the game.

## Part 2

These two texts relate to sport. For questions **19–22**, choose the answer (**A**, **B**, **C** or **D**) which you think fits best according to the text.

### THE BEST REFEREE IN THE WORLD

I am delighted to see that the Italian referee, Pierluigi Collina, has once more been voted the best in the world. Ever since I saw him face down a gesticulating player by approaching to within millimetres of him and daring him to move closer, I have had nothing but admiration for him.

What could possibly induce anyone to become a referee? Surely it's enough to have to put up with foul-mouthed players cheating all the time, managers who refuse to admit any transgressions at one end while protesting bitterly about those at the other, spectators jeering your every mistake (or any award against their team). Yet on top of that, there is a whole host of television commentators waiting to pounce on your errors and, if they were players themselves, calling you harsh whenever you send a player off.

Collina points out that referees are bound to make mistakes that the cameras pick up and are replayed in slow motion. They have one pair of eyes, while the cameras can focus from many angles. But he believes that it is vital for discipline that their decisions should be maintained except when players 'dive', making the

referee believe they have been fouled. In such cases, players should be punished afterwards for the deceit. My personal preference would be a yellow card every time a player commits a cynical foul but then raises his hands above his head in a gesture of injured innocence. But this is why I am not a referee. If I were, there would only be two or three players left on the pitch by the end.

**19**   Which group referred to in the second paragraph are biased in a different way from the others?

   **A**   the players

   **B**   the managers

   **C**   the spectators

   **D**   the commentators

**20**   In what circumstances does Collina think a referee's decision should not be final?

   **A**   If the mistake appears obvious on television.

   **B**   If the mistake is demonstrated by a different camera angle.

   **C**   If a player wrongly convinced him that another had broken the rules.

   **D**   If a player pretended that he had done nothing wrong.

### THE RIGHT AND LEFT FOR SPORTSMEN AND WOMEN

Even in a top-class football match, we often see a player receive a perfect pass in front of the goal but in the split second that it takes for him to transfer the ball to his favourite foot, a defender gets back to frustrate him and the opportunity goes begging. According to sports psychologists, who point out that children playing the piano have better co-ordination between the two sides of the body, this happens far more often than it should, so they are developing training programmes to counteract it.

Something like 85% of us are right-handed and about the same proportion right-footed but, in a game like football, it must surely be an advantage to be able to use each foot with the same effectiveness. All the same, being equally at ease with left or right is nevertheless more important in some sports than others. In racket sports like tennis, the stronger the one hand that is used the better.

As usual in any scientific investigation, there are discordant voices. A professor at London University thinks the time spent on equating left with right would be far better spent perfecting the stronger side. His research is based on a study of chimpanzees, who are not predominantly right-handed but tend to use one hand most of the time. For what it's worth, I suspect the professor is onto something for left-footed players. There are not very many of them, so the more skilful they become with that foot, the better their chances of getting to the top.

**21**　Why does the player described in the first paragraph fail to score?

　　**A**　poor technique

　　**B**　slow reactions

　　**C**　reliance on one foot to shoot

　　**D**　poor co-ordination between his feet

**22**　What does the writer think of the university professor's view?

　　**A**　It is irrelevant, being based on a study of monkeys.

　　**B**　It makes more sense than that of the psychologists.

　　**C**　It is the right approach for the majority of sports people.

　　**D**　It is the right approach for a minority.

---

**Active Vocabulary List**

These are some words and phrases closely connected with the subject of sport. If you are not sure of the meaning of any words or phrases, look them up in your dictionary.

| | |
|---|---|
| sport, game, match, race | tennis/basketball/baseball player |
| athlete, cyclist, jockey | footballer, golfer, swimmer |
| team, side, captain | field, pitch, court, pool, gym |
| ground, stadium | spectator, fan, supporter, hooligan |
| referee, umpire, judge | score, goal, point, set, tie break, final score |
| racket, club, oar, stick | win, lose, draw, tie |

## Part 3 (Ordering paragraphs)

This article consists of 15 paragraphs. Seven of them have been removed. Choose from the paragraphs **A-H** the one that fits each gap (**23-29**). There is one extra paragraph that does not fit and which you do not need to use.

### NEW BOULES, PLEASE: A FRENCH TRADITION ENTERS A NEW AGE

The plump grey-bearded man in the Hawaiian shirt and faded jeans squatted in the dirt, his face blank, as if he were bored. *'Allez, le vieux* (Go to it, old man),' shouted one of his team-mates, no youngster himself. Slowly, the old man, cigarette gripped between his lips, rose half upright and flipped his arm. A small silver ball, previously concealed in his fist, zoomed an unlikely distance into the air.

**23** [                    ]

Imagine an international sports contest in which many of the competitors smoke while playing. Imagine a televised global championship that is fought out mostly on the gravelled paths between the lawns in a municipal park. Imagine a world cup, attracting 3,000 teams from 13 countries, in which contestants, male and female, range in age from 80 to 12.

**24** [                    ]

Petanque, for those who have never stayed on a French camp site, is the most popular form of boules, the Gallic version of bowls. It can be played almost anywhere. Efforts are under way to give the sport a professional status and also to win recognition as an Olympic sport.

**25** [                    ]

He went on to complain, however, that the Parisians are winning all the prizes these days because 'they go to bed at nine o'clock, while we in Marseilles stay up talking until midnight.' Not simply talking, if one is to judge by some of the local boules-bellies in competition this week.

**26** [                    ]

Yet despite being a quintessentially French activity, petanque is en route to conquering the world, like football and golf. It is now the most popular sport in the Thai army and a common morale-building activity for Japanese executives.

**27** [                    ]

If you strolled a little way to another quarter final, involving *le vieux* and his friends on a path between the plane trees, you could have been in any village square in Provence. Here the uniform was straw hats, flat caps, garish shirts and scruffy trousers – but still no berets.

**28** [                    ]

'If you win here, you're famous for ever,' he said. 'As you walk down the street, you will hear people say: "Look! There is the man who won the *Mondial de Petanque*!".'

**29** [                    ]

The final, televised nationally for the first time, was won by a team from the Var, the next *departement* to Marseilles. Presumably, they go to bed even earlier there.

*Article by John Litchfield © Independent Newspapers (UK) Ltd*

**A** Petanque differs from other forms of boules because the contestants have to stand still to throw. The name may sound like the noise made when one stainless steel boule strikes another, but it comes from the Provencal phrase *pes tanques*, meaning 'feet planted.'

**B** But *le vieux* will have to wait for fame for another year. His team were eliminated 13-10 in the quarter finals. And the smart-suited favourites from Paris lost in the semi finals.

**C** After re-entering the earth's atmosphere it homed in on an identical ball 3 m away, which it smashed into the middle distance and sporting oblivion. There followed applause and cheers – game and match. '*Bravo, le vieux.*' Kisses all round.

**D** *Le vieux*, alias 60-year-old Andre Chiappe from Marseilles, explained after the match why he was in the competition for the 20th time. It was not for the value of the first prize. Not for the gold medal, nor the trophy.

**E** Eric Bartoli, the local Marseilles champion, denied suggestions that petanque is best played while drunk. 'Petanque is a physical sport like any other. You have to be fit and clear in the head,' he said.

**F** Each contestant in a three-person team has two boules. The team score a point for every boule that ends the game closer to the tiny wooden jack than the nearest boule of the opposing team. The first team to score 13 points wins the match.

**G** Welcome to the *Mondial* – or 'world cup' – *de Petanque*, which ended in a blaze of television lights in Marseilles during the early hours of yesterday. It is the 40th time the event has been contested.

**H** Judging by the style of headgear among contestants and spectators this week, globalism is also well on the way to conquering petanque. The tensest showdown of the week was between Eric Bartoli's team of Marseilles champions and a neatly uniformed team from Paris. There was not one beret to be seen among the crowd, but at least 1,000 baseball caps blossomed.

## Part I

For questions 1–18, read the texts and decide which answer (**A**, **B**, **C** or **D**) best fits each gap.

### WHEN A SPADE IS NOT A SPADE

The authorities have promised to get (1) .............. with firms that trick people by using jargon. But what (2) .............. that heading? Does it only (3) .............. technical terms or does it mean dressing up plain English with euphemisms and refusing to call a spade a spade?

Euphemism – not saying someone is lying, for instance, but merely being '(4) .............. with the truth' – has its proper place. But if it becomes the custom, as it has with lawyers and politicians, the distinction is lost because the terms are taken to mean exactly the same. By all means make (5) .............. of people who use jargon to deceive. But what is really more serious for the future of the language is that it is being impoverished by usage that consistently (6) .............. the real meaning.

| | | | | | | | | |
|---|---|---|---|---|---|---|---|---|
| **1** | **A** | fierce | **B** | hard | **C** | firm | **D** | tough |
| **2** | **A** | comes under | **B** | encompasses | **C** | includes | **D** | takes part in |
| **3** | **A** | apply | **B** | denote | **C** | import | **D** | communicate |
| **4** | **A** | economical | **B** | partial | **C** | incomplete | **D** | insufficient |
| **5** | **A** | an exposure | **B** | a reproach | **C** | an example | **D** | a censure |
| **6** | **A** | reforms | **B** | distorts | **C** | misinterprets | **D** | deteriorates |

### WHEN A SPADE IS NOT A SPADE (CONTINUED)

There is nothing new in plain English being under attack and lawyers, rather than the media, are primarily responsible. Their (7) .............. to demand vast sums to (8) .............. their clients' reputations, supposedly (9) .............. by newspaper articles, makes editors cautious. Even the police (10) .............. to this misuse of language. Suspects are said to be 'helping them with their inquiries', when we know they are doing nothing of the (11) .............. , but saying nothing or (12) .............. every accusation.

| | | | | | | | | |
|---|---|---|---|---|---|---|---|---|
| **7** | **A** | conviction | **B** | reaction | **C** | practice | **D** | readiness |
| **8** | **A** | refresh | **B** | recover | **C** | reinstate | **D** | rebuild |
| **9** | **A** | knocked out | **B** | unmade | **C** | demolished | **D** | overturned |
| **10** | **A** | contribute | **B** | assist | **C** | connive | **D** | insist |
| **11** | **A** | type | **B** | kind | **C** | manner | **D** | form |
| **12** | **A** | denying | **B** | discussing | **C** | objecting | **D** | disagreeing |

## WHICH WAY NEXT FOR TV?

Television executives need to be able to predict shifts in popular taste. In (13) ............... , it may seem obvious that one programme was bound to be a hit, another a flop, but it is much more important to recognise it in (14) ............... .

One pointer in the present situation is that following increased news (15) ............... of a war, viewers may now be less (16) ............... on so-called 'reality shows', in which ordinary people are (17) ............... to unpleasant experiences. Most broadcasters are prepared to (18) ............... on them wanting more of the same thing, but a few argue that it's time to switch to a television that educates and informs.

| | | | | | | | |
|---|---|---|---|---|---|---|---|
| 13 | **A** memory | **B** recollection | **C** remembrance | **D** retrospect |
| 14 | **A** advance | **B** the long run | **C** principle | **D** future |
| 15 | **A** coverage | **B** spread | **C** relation | **D** publicity |
| 16 | **A** eager | **B** enthusiastic | **C** fond | **D** keen |
| 17 | **A** treated | **B** reduced | **C** subjected | **D** undergone |
| 18 | **A** invest | **B** bank | **C** chance | **D** risk |

### Vocabulary Development

Complete the sentences below with a word or phrase taken from the choices for the questions you have answered. The sentences are printed in the same order as the questions. Note the difference between the correct answer below and a phrase of similar meaning in the passages above.

1  The authorities will take a ................................... line with firms that mislead customers.

2  Does the definition only ................................... to technical terms?

3  The practice of replacing plain English with euphemisms will eventually cause the language to .............................. .

4  Their ................................... to any accusation made in the newspapers is to demand compensation.

5  When the accusations against her proved false, the firm were forced to ................................... her as managing director.

6  As usual, the man's lawyers are ................................... to every question we ask him.

7  He kept shaking his head and .................................. with our interpretation of the evidence.

8  The programme may not be successful at first, but in ................................... I'm sure it will be a hit.

9  The public don't seem to be as ................................... about reality shows as they were.

10  The sponsors may not be prepared to ................................... in another programme like that.

## Part 2
These texts deal with different aspects of media and the arts. For questions **19–22**, choose the answer (**A**, **B**, **C** or **D**) which you think fits best according to the text.

## Books of the year

### Alice in Exile
Paul Read combines consummate story-telling with a readiness to confront unfashionable issues, such as good and evil. He has never written more convincingly.

### Sea Room
Works showing genuine love are rare, so Adam Nicolson's is a wonderfully unusual, unfashionable book, an evocation of the history and landscape of islands off the west coast of Scotland.

### The Sceptical Environmentalist
Bjorn Lomborg is a former member of Greenpeace now willing to proclaim the unfashionable truth that the planet is not doomed, and technology is a better friend to the Earth than many primitive societies.

### Them
Fashionable approaches to extremists are to take them with deadly seriousness or try to understand them. Jon Ronson's story of his encounters with them makes one laugh out loud, as well as shudder.

### Iris Murdoch: a Life
Iris Murdoch once told an interviewer that she based all her characters on herself. Peter Conradi's biography shows she meant what she said. She spent the first half of her life living out her romantic fantasies and the second half writing them.

### Atonement
Ian McEwan's novel is a mixture. There are elements of Jane Austen-style romance for the girls, plenty of war for the boys. But if only the first of these appeals to you, and you haven't read it recently, or, dare I say, ever, why not try the real thing – *Emma*?

19 Which of these books is 'unfashionable' because of the opinions it expresses?

A *Alice in Exile*

B *Sea Room*

C *The Sceptical Environmentalist*

D *Them*

20 Based on these recommendations, which book would you give as a present to someone who 'just likes a good love story'?

A *Sea Room*

B *Iris Murdoch: a life*

C *Atonement*

D *Emma*

## A FAVOURITE ACTRESS

A recent interview with Zoe Wanamaker began by saying that she has an untypical face for an actress because she is instantly recognisable. I was reminded of this when I accompanied my grandchildren to *Harry Potter*, where all the adult actors are heavily made up. I saw straightaway that she was the referee in the spectacular scene where Harry and the others play a kind of flying roller-hockey on broomsticks, grey-haired but still very much the same as when she charmed me twenty years ago.

This was at Stratford, when she played the heroine, Viola, in Shakespeare's last great truly romantic comedy, *Twelfth Night*. I was with my wife, who is Spanish, and had refused to tell her anything of the plot beforehand, hoping that she would enjoy the play much more if Shakespeare were left to work his magic. She was convinced that she would not understand a word but afterwards told me it had been a wonderful experience. She had not realised how dramatic Shakespeare is, in the sense that you can understand what is going on even if much of the language escapes you. Privately, my feeling was one of gratitude to the director, Adrian Noble, for letting the play speak for itself, unlike many modern directors, and proving my hunch correct.

Zoe Wanamaker was not quite my idea of Viola and could not have been. Viola is the most feminine, the least boyish of Shakespeare's romantic heroines, bravely keeping up her pretence of manhood but fighting back her tears even when dressed as a boy. Ms Wanamaker had a stronger personality and physique than this, but she impressed with her absolute sincerity, the key to understanding this character in a play where everyone else is playing at being in love, while she stands for the real thing.

21 Why did the writer feel grateful towards the director of *Twelfth Night*?

　A Because he had not altered the language.

　B Because the action was understandable.

　C Because the production was faithful to the text.

　D Because he had not explained the play to his wife.

22 What was the most convincing aspect of Ms Wanamaker's performance for the writer?

　A She personified the most important theme of the play.

　B She looked like his conception of the character.

　C She conveyed the strength of the character.

　D She was very effective when dressed as a boy.

### Active Vocabulary List

These are some words and phrases closely connected with the subject of the media. If you are not sure of the meaning of any words or phrases, look them up in your dictionary.

| | |
|---|---|
| newspaper, magazine | radio, television |
| the press (quality, popular) | channel |
| article, feature, editorial | broadcast, programme, show |
| reporter, journalist, editor | newsreader, presenter |
| readers, circulation | listeners, viewers, viewing figures |
| advertisements, commercials | documentary, series, soap opera |

*Part 3 (Multiple-choice comprehension)*
Read this article about an interview with an actress. For questions **23–29**, choose the answer (**A**, **B**, **C** or **D**) which you think fits best according to the text.

## A JOLLY GOOD SORT

It's a sweltering, steamy London day and a dehydrated horde of city types are lunching as loudly as the steam hammers smashing up the city centre. Olivia Williams, who's chosen the venue because she once had a delightful quiet breakfast there, decides to take matters in hand. 'Could I,' she asks the waiter, her voice ringingly clear and tinklingly authoritative, 'be so bossy as to ask you to turn the music down? And could I be so fussy as to ask for a little lime in my drink? *He's* (she points at me) got some. It's only fair I should.'

She could, with her well-scrubbed cheeks, eccentrically cut white shirt and dark clogs, be a go-getting headmistress or a coming figure in the Liberal Democrat party. Given her background – both parents lawyers and part-time judges, and 'on the liberal wing of the judiciary': secondary education at an academically excellent private school and English at Cambridge – she could easily be either of these things. In fact, she's a first-rate actress, particularly adept at registering the most fleeting emotions with the most finely nuanced facial expressions.

She's got a new film to promote, *Lucky Break*, an engaging prison escape comedy. In it she has a fresh chance to display a remarkable skill. In her two most successful roles to date, she did that difficult thing: play a good person without being nauseating. 'Yes,' she says, 'I unfortunately have, I think, proved myself in Hollywood to be able to deliver the unsayably sugary line with conviction, which isn't necessarily a skill I should have developed so well. I can be very horrible if I want to be. And I can do cow. I really can. I really enjoy it. The baddies have all the best lines. Roll on Lady Macbeth!'

All this is delivered with much gusto and gesturing. 'If you think I'm animated, you should see my mother!' The forehead, flecked by a childhood scar, is allowed to furrow. She wears no make-up. She is determinedly natural. And her remarks, in their breezy candour, are typical of her seeming carelessness of the studios' sensibilities. 'A business that relies on bluster and half-truths,' she'll say of the industry, or, of a scorned project, 'I wasn't particularly excited about being in an inane comedy.' But in contrast: 'I went to see *Lucky Break* with my mates and all the people in the movie, and there was real euphoria, watching what everyone had made together.'

Olivia Williams is at a crucial moment in her career. Despite rolling out a succession of films, she's still best known for something she did four years ago. As an unknown, penniless actress on the verge of jacking in the trade, she refused Kevin Costner's request, made in a personal telephone call, that she tape a second video audition for the lead female role in the film he was making. This obviously impressed him, she got the part, saw the film, *The Postman*, turn into a box-office flop, and flew to her next date with celluloid destiny, *Rushmore*, in Costner's private jet.

Her skills were nurtured at Bristol Old Vic Theatre school, to which she went after Cambridge. She was, she says, never convinced – 'and I'm still not' – that she would make a career out of acting. For years, she seemed to have been right. She served her time in rep. at Westcliff-on-Sea, did good work with the Royal Shakespeare Company, elicited a rave review for a television role as Jane Fairfax in *Emma*, but pre-Costner was mostly flogging a dead horse.

Her career trajectory is certainly odd. Her big breaks have taken place in America but she has, through choice, followed them with a slew of lowish-budget British movies. It's not as if she's unwanted in Hollywood or looks down her nose at it. It's merely that she can't bring herself to leave her London home because her parents live within sight and the cycle paths are so good. Even Marylebone, a mere mile away, makes her feel 'homesick and pathetic.'

For all the openness and jollity, there's a paid-up performer in Williams. She got the bug early, she thinks she has it in her genes. Her elder sister, who's a solicitor, hasn't. 'She's got the more responsible reserve. I've got the youngest-child show-off gene.' It's a slightly bumptious gene, too. 'My mother's delivery in court is really dry and monotonous. She was going to present a case before the European court and I said, "Frankly, your speaking voice could do with a bit of perking up."'

Olivia Williams oozes certainty and conviction. She says she has a strong sense of morality, one that 'can be misread as judgemental, prim, holier than thou.' But she admits to one fault. She can be deliberately unreasonable. That is what caused her to say 'no' to Kevin Costner, not calculation or dizziness. That time it paid off but there are times when the studio says: 'Fly out tomorrow,' and she says: 'I'm sorry, but I've got something else to do. It's my father's birthday or I have an appointment at the hairdresser's and I don't choose to break it.'

No wonder Kevin Costner crumbled before her. She is both a brilliant actress and the sort of woman behind whom anyone would march into the jungle. Or almost anyone. As Williams adds: 'So sometimes I didn't get on the plane and I didn't get the job. Sometimes you end up in Hollywood, and sometimes you don't.'

*Article by David Jenkins © Telegraph Group Limited*

**23**    The actress complained to the waiter because of

    **A**    the heat.

    **B**    the noise outside.

    **C**    the noise inside.

    **D**    the choice of music.


**24**    Why is the actress's skill described as 'remarkable' in the third paragraph?

    **A**    Because good characters in films usually sound unreal.

    **B**    Because she regrets the ability she has developed.

    **C**    Because she has excelled in roles quite different from her own personality.

    **D**    Because the tragic roles are the most interesting ones.


**25**    Which of these phrases in the fourth paragraph suggests that Olivia Williams cannot help playing a part, even in the interview?

    **A**    'much gusto and gesturing'

    **B**    'determinedly natural'

    **C**    'breezy candour'

    **D**    'bluster and half-truths'


**26**    What caused Kevin Costner to offer her a starring role?

    **A**    He felt sorry for her because she was on the point of abandoning her career.

    **B**    He was astonished that she turned the part down at first.

    **C**    Her belief that what he had already seen of her was enough.

    **D**    The first film she made with him was a great success.


**27**    Why is her career so far described as 'odd'? *(paragraph 7)*

    **A**    Because she became an actress despite being so well educated.

    **B**    Because she has never believed she would succeed.

    **C**    Because she despises Hollywood, where she has been successful.

    **D**    Because she seems to regard it as secondary to her personal life.


**28**    What does Olivia Williams say about acting and the family?

    **A**    Acting is part of a family tradition.

    **B**    It comes naturally to anyone whose family are lawyers.

    **C**    Younger daughters are more likely to become actresses.

    **D**    She takes after her mother.


**29**    Which of these adjectives best describes Olivia Williams' personality, in the interviewer's opinion?

    **A**    self-confident

    **B**    narrow minded

    **C**    awkward

    **D**    fatalistic

**Part I**

For questions 1–18, read the texts and decide which answer (**A**, **B**, **C** or **D**) best fits each gap.

---

### THE DISCOVERY OF MACHU PICCHU

A dramatic moment in archaeological history occurred in 1911, when the American explorer Hiram Bingham first (1) ............... on this Inca city in Peru. Yet the discovery occurred by accident when Bingham's guide invited him to take a (2) ............... at it from the top of a nearby hill. His companions were too tired to accompany him, so he reached the summit alone, (3) ............... dumb with wonder.

Nevertheless, he does not appear to have taken in the importance of what he had seen at first. He (4) ............... little to his companions and did not revisit the site until a year later. In his account of the adventure, now out of (5) ............... and no longer obtainable, he imagined it as a refuge from the Spanish invaders, but documents suggest that it was the country retreat of an Inca ruler, (6) ............... before the conquest.

---

| 1 | **A** caught sight | **B** had a vision | **C** set eyes | **D** stole a glance |
|---|---|---|---|---|
| 2 | **A** look | **B** sight | **C** view | **D** watch |
| 3 | **A** shocked | **B** turned | **C** struck | **D** knocked |
| 4 | **A** told | **B** said | **C** spoke | **D** recounted |
| 5 | **A** publication | **B** print | **C** edition | **D** stock |
| 6 | **A** abandoned | **B** detached | **C** disowned | **D** relegated |

---

### MORE FLOODS OR THE SAME AS USUAL?

The popular press and politicians often get excited about the British weather, the former to find a scapegoat, the latter to ensure that none of the blame rubs off on them. So the Minister of Labour recently (7) ............... more floods because of global warming. But there have always been floods and always will be. All that happens is that (8) ............... , in autumn and winter, more weather systems than usual cross the Atlantic. The (9) ............... rain falls in the west and north and this finds its (10) ............... into the rivers that flood the plains further south and east.

If floods do more damage today it is because developers, successfully (11) ............... to local councils to overturn planning decisions, build houses on (12) ............... sites. Instead of blaming global warming, the Minister ought to put a stop to this building and introduce sanctions against the councils.

---

| 7 | **A** previewed | **B** forecast | **C** advertised | **D** menaced |
|---|---|---|---|---|
| 8 | **A** uncommonly | **B** occasionally | **C** scarcely | **D** infrequently |
| 9 | **A** strongest | **B** greatest | **C** heaviest | **D** biggest |
| 10 | **A** course | **B** direction | **C** passage | **D** way |
| 11 | **A** appealing | **B** submitting | **C** demanding | **D** entreating |
| 12 | **A** inadequate | **B** improper | **C** misplaced | **D** unsuitable |

---

**ARE SPORTS STARS ABOVE THE LAW?**

The managers' reaction after the rioting at the football match at Cardiff last weekend was only too predictable. The Leeds manager, two of whose players had a (13) .............. escape from a prison sentence not long ago, described the crowd's behaviour as disgusting. The Cardiff manager, in (14) .............. of his more famous counterparts, who are blind to any thuggery their players indulge in either on or off the pitch, saw nothing to be (15) .............. of. In his view, the violence was just 'passionate fans enjoying themselves.'

Meanwhile two London players were under (16) .............. for attacking staff at a night club. Before long we may find a footballer literally '(17) .............. with murder.' The reasons are obvious. They are popular idols whose fans cannot (18) .............. to think they could do anything wrong.

---

| | | | | | | | | |
|---|---|---|---|---|---|---|---|---|
| **13** | **A** | close | **B** | slight | **C** | narrow | **D** | marginal |
| **14** | **A** | parallel | **B** | imitation | **C** | reflection | **D** | duplication |
| **15** | **A** | ashamed | **B** | upset | **C** | objected | **D** | shocked |
| **16** | **A** | accusation | **B** | arrest | **C** | trial | **D** | detention |
| **17** | **A** | getting away | **B** | getting off | **C** | making away | **D** | making off |
| **18** | **A** | stand | **B** | support | **C** | endure | **D** | bear |

**Tip**

*You have one hour 30 minutes to complete the whole test. Do not spend too long on any one part, and remember that questions **1-18** are worth one mark, questions **19-40** are worth two!*

## Part 2

You are going to read four extracts on different topics. For questions **19–26**, choose the answer (**A, B, C** or **D**) which you think fits best according to the text.

### GHOST STORIES AT CHRISTMAS

Ghost stories seem to be coming back into fashion, both in books and in the cinema, and ever since the Victorians developed the form, Christmas has been the favourite time for telling them. There is something oddly cosy about sitting around a warm fire in semi-darkness, listening to things that make your flesh creep. And the film, *The Others*, starring Nicole Kidman, contains all the classic elements – a remote house cut off from the world by fog, a mother convinced that her children are in danger from supernatural forces, sinister servants, doors that creak and heavy footsteps upstairs.

The mother's concern for her children in *The Others* echoes the most famous of all ghost stories in English, Henry James' *The Turn of the Screw*. But James' story is appalling where *The Others* is not because it is ambiguous. Even at the end, we do not know whether the ghosts were the malignant spirits of former servants, trying to entice the children into the next world, or the products of their governess's neurotic imagination.

19  Which of the following best summarises the content of the first paragraph
    **A**  Ghost stories have always been popular.
    **B**  Ghost stories relate to Christmas.
    **C**  It is strange that ghost stories attract us by scaring us.
    **D**  The traditional appeal of ghost stories remains unchanged.

20  What makes *The Turn of the Screw* such a frightening story?
    **A**  We are not sure if what we are told is true.
    **B**  The ghosts are evil, unlike those in *The Others*.
    **C**  The ghosts are threatening children.
    **D**  The person who tells the story is mad.

## AVALANCHE

An avalanche rushing down a mountain is one of the most spectacular sights nature affords, provided you are viewing it from a safe distance. If you are caught up in it, it is at best terrifying, at worst lethal. Avalanches kill over 150 people every year and the toll is increasing as winter sports become more popular, above all when longer days tempt more people into the mountains and warmer weather begins to melt the snow. The conventional picture of an avalanche shows it suddenly thundering down onto the heads of unsuspecting villagers, but far more often the victim or someone in the victim's party is responsible.

In countries with long experience of coping with avalanches, the body of information built up should reduce the risks. This information also extends to advice on equipment and how to react if you are unlucky enough to be caught. Skiers have a better chance of survival if they have time to inflate airbags as protection against being buried in the snow. Most survivors have been dug out within half an hour and no one has lived under it for much longer. The most useful action to perform is to throw away your backpack and ski sticks, and imitate swimming, trying to stay near the surface of the snow. When the avalanche stops, you will have a few seconds to punch an air hole in the snow before it freezes over you. It is worth remembering that many victims of avalanches choke to death before they die of cold.

21    What is indicated as the main cause of avalanches?

    **A**    the increasing popularity of winter sports

    **B**    people skiing at the wrong time of year

    **C**    a natural phenomenon

    **D**    human error

22    Which of the following represents the skier's first priority in an avalanche?

    **A**    carrying the correct equipment

    **B**    keeping warm

    **C**    getting rid of equipment that is not needed

    **D**    being able to breathe

---

### SPORTS ROUND-UP

#### Motor rallying

Defending champion Jutta Kleinschmidt won the 10th stage of the Paris-Dakar rally yesterday to keep up the pressure on race leader Hiroshi Matsuoka. The German driver, the first woman to win the event, is still 20 minutes behind overall.

#### Basketball

Cup finalists Chester and Birmingham are hit by injuries prior to Sunday's match. Chester wait to see if Hamilton has recovered from an ankle injury while Birmingham's Garcia suffered a broken ankle against Derby.

#### American Football

Emmitt Smith stole the spotlight in the final game in Detroit, becoming the first player in National Football League history to gain over 1,000 yards in 11 consecutive seasons.

#### Squash

British champion Lee Beachill was, for a second time, unable to complete his opening match in Boston. After a delay for technical reasons yesterday, he had to quit halfway through his match because of heat exhaustion brought on by 'flu.

#### Rugby Union

Coventry have asked the RFU to award them full points after Birmingham's refusal to play last Saturday. The referee ruled the pitch playable, but the game was called off an hour before kick-off when the Birmingham captain claimed the surface was still frozen.

#### Motor racing

The Prost Formula One racing team may have their future guaranteed by a group of French businessmen, willing to put up 45 million euros. They met Prost last Thursday, and are expected to become majority shareholders.

---

**23**   Which paragraph refers to a match terminated by illness?

    **A**   Motor rallying

    **B**   Squash

    **C**   Basketball

    **D**   Rugby Union

**24**   Which paragraphs refer to unprecedented achievements in sport?

    **A**   Motor rallying and Squash

    **B**   Motor rallying and American Football

    **C**   Squash and Motor racing

    **D**   American Football and Motor racing

## CARY GRANT

The National Film Theatre is about to launch a long film season dedicated to the work of Cary Grant, and in his native city of Bristol a statue is to be unveiled to this archetypal Hollywood star, the epitome of upper-class sophistication, born in a working-class district as Archibald Leach and trained in boyhood as a circus acrobat. His reinvention of himself once he had crossed the Atlantic, reputedly stowing away on a cargo ship, was in itself extraordinary, but what is still a cause for wonder is how successfully he lived up to his adopted image.

The truth is that he was a consummate professional in everything he did, gifted with supreme self-assurance, which enabled him to tackle a variety of roles – not all of them were comic – without ever needing to hog the limelight or battle with his co-star. As he was on the screen, so he was off. He retired at 62, never attempted a comeback, never stooped to writing intimate memoirs, never accepted invitations to be interviewed on television, never authorised a biography. His private persona showed the same discretion as his personality in films. There his charm lay in always appearing approachable and one of us, yet at the same time touched with an indefinable source of glamour that set him apart – in short, he was a star.

25  What was the most astonishing feature of Cary Grant's reinvention of himself?

  **A**  The contrast between his real name and his adopted one.

  **B**  The contrast between his background and screen personality.

  **C**  His ability to adapt to his new social role so effectively.

  **D**  The fact that he was British but became a Hollywood star.

26  Which of the actions other film stars have undertaken in retirement does the writer clearly disapprove of?

  **A**  returning to the screen

  **B**  writing about their private lives

  **C**  helping journalists to write about them

  **D**  appearing on chat shows

## Part 3

This article consists of 15 paragraphs. Seven of them have been removed. Choose from the paragraphs **A–H** the one that fits each gap (**27–33**). There is one extra paragraph that does not fit and which you do not need to use.

### INDIANA JONES ... AND THE LOST SCOUT

In a flamboyant case of life imitating art, Harrison Ford has been hailed as a hero after mounting a rescue mission worthy of his alter ego, Indiana Jones. The 58-year-old actor took to the skies in his Bell 407 helicopter in search of a boy scout who was reported lost in Yellowstone National Park.

| 27 | |
|---|---|

Ford, who last year airlifted an exhausted hiker from a mountain top, is not the only performer who can't quite shake off his on-screen persona. Earlier this week, 16-year-old *Sopranos* actor Robert Iler appeared in court on robbery and drugs charges.

| 28 | |
|---|---|

Being identified with any long-running role is of course an occupational hazard. Method actors such as Marlon Brando and Daniel Day-Lewis are famous for inhabiting their characters on and off-set when preparing for a performance.

| 29 | |
|---|---|

'I was walking past when a man shouted "She's a nurse. She'll help you," ' she says. 'I said, "I'm sorry, I've got no medical training," and started to go, but everybody began saying "Look, she's a nurse, and she's just walking away," and I was so embarrassed I turned back.'

| 30 | |
|---|---|

Like actors who play doctors or nurses, anyone who portrays a police officer runs the risk of being called on in a crisis. Graham Cole, who plays PC Tony Stamp in *The Bill*, says he is wary of being regarded as a real copper after hours.

| 31 | |
|---|---|

'There was one occasion when I defused a punch-up in a pizza place,' he says. 'There were two rival gangs of 15- or 16-year-olds about to lay into each other but when I walked through the door, they just stopped dead and said, "Hey, it's *The Bill*." '

| 32 | |
|---|---|

In a fracas at the anti-capitalist demonstrations in London in May, former *Juliet Bravo* actress Anna Carteret found the recognition factor worked in her favour. Carteret, who has always been politically radical, was marching along Oxford Street when she found herself hemmed in by police barriers.

| 33 | |
|---|---|

If actors fear their careers are coming to an end, they clearly need a selling point that sets them apart. Harrison Ford has just signed an £18 million deal for the next *Indiana Jones* film. What better promotional tool for the producers than a dashing male lead who spends his spare time rescuing boy scouts from the woods?

*Article by Judith Woods © Telegraph Group Limited*

**A**   But some professionals find themselves unable to shake off public perceptions, with potentially alarming consequences. Sunetra Sarker, 28, who plays the femme fatale nurse Nisha in *Brookside*, was leaving a theatre with friends when a woman collapsed.

**B**   Drivers regularly flag him down and inquire about parking restrictions. In pubs, fellow drinkers ask whether he thinks they're over the limit. And once, in a restaurant, when someone started to choke, all eyes turned to him to cope with the situation, which he fortunately managed to do.

**C**   Whenever actors do anything out of the ordinary, they may be seen by others as crossing the boundaries between their role and reality. But those who admire them are far more likely to make assumptions that aren't necessarily true.

**D**   She held the woman's hand and said, 'I'm Sunetra. Can you hear me?' Fortunately she responded and opened her eyes. 'I was surrounded by all these people saying "See! You can do it. You are a nurse," even though I'd done absolutely nothing.'

**E**   Ever the professional, he had a laconic line ready for when he finally tracked down 13-year-old Cody Clawson. 'You sure must have earned a badge from this one,' was the wisecrack that greeted the stunned schoolboy.

**F**   Together with the rest of the crowd she was held for five hours. As the mood grew increasingly frustrated, a passing policeman recognised her as the former Inspector Langton, and discreetly allowed her out, saying, 'he trusted her not to be violent.'

**G**   The actor, who plays tearaway Anthony Jr, the son of Mafia boss Tony Soprano, was one of three teenagers arrested in Manhattan after an alleged mugging. Unlike the others, however, he was flanked by three public relations experts keen on damage limitation.

**H**   But he admits that after 16 years in the series, people respond to him as they would to a genuine policeman. And when he gives talks in schools and youth centres as part of crime prevention initiatives, teenagers often regard him as more credible than the real thing.

## Part 4

You are going to read an article about fans who watch sport from an armchair. For questions **34–40**, choose the answer (**A**, **B**, **C** or **D**) which you think fits best according to the text.

### THE ARMCHAIR SPORTS FAN

Let's start with the hardware. This weekend around 50 backsides in Britain are luxuriating in the leathery embrace of the La-Z-Boy Oasis recliner, the 'ultimate sports fan's armchair', which comes with a built-in electric beer cooler, a massage and heating system, and which, for a suitable premium over its basic price tag, can be ordered in the livery of the owner's favourite team. Their success, according to the firm's marketing boss, is due to the fact that 'Sports fans don't just want a place to sit. They need a genuinely understanding chair.'

And a genuinely understanding family. Life used to be relatively simple for sofa-bound sports fans. All you had to do was to open the bottles of beer and endure the drivel of the commentators with reasonable grace. Television sport – at least of a calibre above moto-cross – was a fairly occasional treat. But things have changed, with profound consequences both for sport and society. There is now a mass of live sport – not just recorded highlights – and something somewhere in the world is always happening.

But here's the paradox; as more people follow sport on television, fewer are up to participating in it for real. The streets of Britain are awash with premature physical wrecks dressed, without any sense of irony, in expensive trainers and designer track suits. The average town centre looks like an Olympic warm-up zone. But we are fatter and less active than any generation in history and we haul this clobber into pubs, where grown men in soccer shirts howl like dogs at television sets.

The armchair sports fan is no mug, though. He has served his time on the soccer terraces and the cricket ground. Most likely the race track, too. And he knows that what he once believed about bearing first-hand witness to live sport is so much guff. He's had enough of shivering in the rain while the local low-lifes steal his car radio. On occasion, he may have splashed out for a ticket to a grand prix and wondered why all he saw was a flash as the drivers zipped past. Above all he has learned that his eyes and ears and any other sentient resources he can muster are no match for the awesome technological wizardry television now brings to sports coverage.

The armchair sports fan knows, therefore, exactly why it is better to watch at home. Even if he ends up with a divorce, he doesn't want to miss out on anything important. The camera now takes him to places he could otherwise never dream of going to. There are cameras in golf holes and in jockeys' hats.

Television sport isn't so much staged as choreographed. Sports that were once thought to be beyond the reach of television, like ocean racing or rock climbing, have been turned into authentic spectacles by the ingenuity of the camera.

But the techno-wonders of the armchair age don't end there. Digital television already allows viewers to choose camera angles, replays and highlights. But how about this for advanced armchair viewing? Japanese technicians have invented a video recorder with action-sensitive software that will automatically cut out the dull parts of any sporting fixture. And it's all for the benefit of the (typically) 30-50-year-old, sedentary, semi-skilled or lower middle class male with a packet of crisps, an England football shirt and looming marital problems.

Or is it? Sport as big business is so recent a phenomenon that the pure economics of it are still evolving. All the armchair fan really needs to know, vaguely, is that he'll be paying the bill. The modern era of commercialisation really began in the rancorous aftermath of the 1976 Montreal Olympics, which left Canada with a financial deficit so huge it almost toppled the country's government. Eight years later, when the games arrived in Los Angeles, the lessons had been learned.

The LA committee packaged the games up and sold them to the highest bidders. The television networks were ruthlessly played off against each other for the maximum possible payout. The financial result was as spectacular as Montreal's was embarrassing, and sport has never been the same since. Everyone now knew where the real money was to be made, and it wasn't from a handful of diehards in the stadium.

Now the armchair fan is king. Promoters defer to him, athletes pay homage to him, companies understand the urgent need to involve him. No one can be sure what the consequences will be. Family campaigners fear rises in divorce rates, the collapse of community cohesion, and the further detachment of children reared on a neat diet of televised sport.

One inescapable effect of this is the rise of the self-made expert, the man who couldn't sink a putt from 10 cm but will tell you that Tiger Woods is playing the wrong shot. But where will it end? Where else is there for the cameras to go? Will they follow the players home to bed? Still, there is one thing the armchair sports fan can be sure of: increased comfort. La-Z-Boy's next model will probably have an optional heated pizza tray.

© Telegraph Group Limited

**34**  Why does the armchair sports fan need 'a genuinely understanding family'. *(Paragraph 2, first sentence)*

    **A**  Because he spends so much money on sport.

    **B**  Because he spends so much time watching sport.

    **C**  Because he spends so much on personal comfort.

    **D**  Because he needs their sympathy when his team lose.

**35**  What does the change the writer is describing in the second paragraph consist of?

    **A**  People used to go out to watch sport, instead of staying at home.

    **B**  The broadcasts are more intelligent than they used to be.

    **C**  The more interesting sports never used to be shown.

    **D**  There are now many more sports options to choose from on TV.

**36**  What is the irony that the sports fans described in the third paragraph are unaware of?

    **A**  They watch sport but no longer take part in it.

    **B**  They enjoy watching sport despite their poor state of health.

    **C**  The clothes they wear are totally inappropriate.

    **D**  They are well dressed but behave badly.

**37**  What is the main advantage for sports fans watching it at home?

    **A**  They can see much better.

    **B**  They avoid bad weather.

    **C**  There is no chance of being robbed.

    **D**  It is cheaper.

**38**  Which of the sports fan's problems does the latest invention aim to deal with?

    **A**  seeing what has happened from a different angle

    **B**  seeing what has happened several times

    **C**  being bored

    **D**  involving the rest of the family in the activity

**39**  What was the main cause of the transformation that has produced the modern armchair sports fan?

    **A**  The TV companies could now afford to provide greater variety.

    **B**  Political considerations following the 1976 Olympic Games.

    **C**  The realisation that the fans would pay any price they were asked.

    **D**  Competition between TV companies to attract audiences for sports events.

**40**  What point is the writer making about armchair sports fans in the last paragraph?

    **A**  That after watching so much sport they think they know more than world champions.

    **B**  That they are so curious about the lives of sports people that they want to see them off the field.

    **C**  That by this time there is nothing more that can be offered to them.

    **D**  That all they really care about is comfort, rather than sport.

*Phrasal verbs*

**A**    Rewrite the sentences, using the correct phrasal verb from the list in the correct tense.

| bring up | cast aside | live up to | make out | pay off | point out | set off ✓ | stand for | take in | turn out |
|---|---|---|---|---|---|---|---|---|---|

**1**    What time does she usually *start her journey* for the office in the morning?
   *What time does she usually set off for the office in the morning?*

**2**    What do the initials UNO *represent*?
   ......................................................................................................................................................

**3**    They have *abandoned* the old methods *as useless* and are employing new ones.
   ......................................................................................................................................................

**4**    His writing is so bad that it is impossible to *understand* what he is saying.
   ......................................................................................................................................................

**5**    You can't expect the class to *absorb* so many difficult concepts all at once.
   ......................................................................................................................................................

**6**    I hope you won't mind if I *indicate* the mistakes you have made.
   ......................................................................................................................................................

**7**    The royal children were not *looked after and taught how to behave* by their parents.
   ......................................................................................................................................................

**8**    He was a great disappointment to his parents, and failed to *behave so as to justify* their expectations.
   ......................................................................................................................................................

**9**    The work *proved* to be more difficult than we had imagined.
   ......................................................................................................................................................

**10**    We knew we were taking a risk, but luckily the gamble *proved successful*.
   ......................................................................................................................................................

**B**    Rewrite the sentences, using the correct phrasal verb from the list in the correct tense.

| back out of | break down | break out | crop up | hold out | run into | set out | speak out | split up | turn up |
|---|---|---|---|---|---|---|---|---|---|

**1**    I was wondering if anyone I knew would *appear* at the meeting.
   ......................................................................................................................................................

**2**    She was once married but the marriage *collapsed* after three days!
   ......................................................................................................................................................

**3**    The prospective buyers of the house *withdrew from* the deal when the owners raised the price.
   ......................................................................................................................................................

**4**    If you've been badly treated, *say what you think openly*. Don't keep it to yourself.
   ......................................................................................................................................................

**5**   Problems in teenagers' relationships with their parents often *appear unexpectedly*.

   .........................................................................................................................................................

**6**   The twins depended on each other so much that they resented being *separated*.

   .........................................................................................................................................................

**7**   The Second World War *started* in 1939.

   .........................................................................................................................................................

**8**   She *left that place* the next morning in search of the truth.

   .........................................................................................................................................................

**9**   We *met* each other *quite by accident* at the railway station.

   .........................................................................................................................................................

**10**   I bought just enough food and drink for the party, and it *lasted* till the end.

   .........................................................................................................................................................

**C**   Rewrite the sentences, using the correct phrasal verb from the list in the correct tense.

| come about | cope with | die down | dress up | hack out | make up for | put out | send back | set up | spring up |
|---|---|---|---|---|---|---|---|---|---|

**1**   We are short staffed at the moment and cannot *manage* that amount of work.

   .........................................................................................................................................................

**2**   It's an informal party. There's no need to *put on your best clothes*.

   .........................................................................................................................................................

**3**   I can't imagine how the misunderstanding *happened*.

   .........................................................................................................................................................

**4**   The sports facilities at the hotel *compensated for* the bad weather we had on holiday.

   .........................................................................................................................................................

**5**   The minister waited for the noise to *become less loud* before going on with his speech.

   .........................................................................................................................................................

**6**   The cheque was *returned* because he had no money in his account.

   .........................................................................................................................................................

**7**   The Government are going to *establish* a committee to inquire into the complaints.

   .........................................................................................................................................................

**8**   Shops selling mobile phones are *suddenly appearing* all over the place.

   .........................................................................................................................................................

**9**   The explorers *cut out* a *rough* path through the jungle.

   .........................................................................................................................................................

**10**   The World Cup committee were *upset* to discover that they were not all staying at the same hotel.

   .........................................................................................................................................................

**D**    Rewrite the sentences, using the correct phrasal verb from the list in the correct tense.

> claw back   come up with   do away with   flag down   hang on to   hold up   miss out on   put up   put up with   rub off on

**1**    We had no idea of how to deal with the problem until she *produced* this clever solution.
.......................................................................................................................................................................

**2**    Though he talks of retiring, he'll *hold on tightly to* power for as long as he can.
.......................................................................................................................................................................

**3**    The firm's improved prospects have enabled investors to *recover* some of their losses.
.......................................................................................................................................................................

**4**    The minister appeared at the meeting with a sheep dog, hoping some of its lovable qualities would *be transferred to* him.
.......................................................................................................................................................................

**5**    Please *raise* your hand if you want to ask a question.
.......................................................................................................................................................................

**6**    I was tired of waiting for the bus, so I *waved to* a taxi *to make it stop*.
.......................................................................................................................................................................

**7**    By failing to send in the questionnaire, I *lost the opportunity of* a free holiday abroad.
.......................................................................................................................................................................

**8**    The Post Office has decided to *cancel* the second delivery of the day.
.......................................................................................................................................................................

**9**    It's a disgrace, and I don't see why I should *tolerate* it any longer.
.......................................................................................................................................................................

**10**    The traffic was *kept waiting* for half an hour by the lorry being double-parked.
.......................................................................................................................................................................

**E**    Rewrite the sentences, using the correct phrasal verb from the list in the correct tense.

> break up   call off   cut off   fall off   get away with   keep up   put off   rule out   splash out   wipe out

**1**    The reports of violence in the country *stopped* tourists *being interested in* visiting it.
.......................................................................................................................................................................

**2**    We would be unwilling to *exclude* any reasonable explanation for what happened.
.......................................................................................................................................................................

**3**    There was a lot of interest in the course at first, but numbers have *decreased* recently.
.......................................................................................................................................................................

**4**    Our campaign to *eliminate* the disease *completely* has achieved partial success.
.......................................................................................................................................................................

**5** The schools have *closed for the holidays*, so the children are all at home.

...................................................................................................................................................................

**6** You can't *escape unpunished for* murder, even if you are a famous sportsman.

...................................................................................................................................................................

**7** It was a cause for celebration so we decided to *spend a lot of money* on a meal at an expensive restaurant.

...................................................................................................................................................................

**8** The village has been *separated* from the world by the floods.

...................................................................................................................................................................

**9** Their victory enables them to *maintain* their challenge for the championship.

...................................................................................................................................................................

**10** The game was *cancelled* at the last minute because of ice on the pitch.

...................................................................................................................................................................

**F** Rewrite the sentences, using the correct phrasal verb from the list in the correct tense.

| bank on | bowl over | catch up with | end up | make up | stand up to | stow away | strike down | while away | work out |

**1** Everyone was *astonished and impressed* by the force of her personality.

...................................................................................................................................................................

**2** Women *account for* 90% of the work force.

...................................................................................................................................................................

**3** He joined the firm as an office boy and *finished his career* as managing director.

...................................................................................................................................................................

**4** It's an interesting theory but I doubt if it will *remain valid under* close examination.

...................................................................................................................................................................

**5** She keeps fit by *doing physical training* every morning

...................................................................................................................................................................

**6** I had a long wait at the airport so I *relaxed and passed* the time doing crossword puzzles.

...................................................................................................................................................................

**7** While on holiday he was *infected and incapacitated* by a mysterious illness.

...................................................................................................................................................................

**8** He got into the country by *climbing aboard and hiding* on a ship.

...................................................................................................................................................................

**9** The evil life he has led will *overtake* him *and cause him trouble* one day.

...................................................................................................................................................................

**10** They say it will be fine tomorrow but after looking at those clouds, I wouldn't *be very confident of* it.

...................................................................................................................................................................

## Collocations (1)

G   Complete the sentences with the correct preposition(s).

1   I couldn't have managed by myself. It was a good thing you were .............. hand to help out.
2   You may not think so now but .............. the long run you'll be grateful for my advice.
3   They fell in love .............. first sight.
4   The trouble with the minister is that he's .............. touch with public opinion.
5   It was a sensible proposal so we were all .............. agreement.
6   There's a policeman .............. duty at the crossroads.
7   He refused to answer questions when he appeared .............. court.
8   He acts very strangely. I'm not sure that he's .............. his right mind.
9   He raised his gun to fire but the bird was already .............. range.
10  The public have a right to know these things. They should not be kept .............. ignorance.

## Collocations (2)

H   Complete the sentences with the correct preposition(s).

1   They used to be very common birds but their numbers are ................. decline.
2   That problem is very common. Your brother's experience is a case ................. point.
3   He was a rebel, ................. contrast to his father, a judge.
4   The ship hit a rock and sank ................. trace.
5   It's the first time that these animals have been bred ................. captivity.
6   They set off ................. pursuit of the thieves.
7   They insist on the rent being paid ................. advance.
8   You are ................. arrest and anything you say may be used against you.
9   It seemed right at the time, but ................. retrospect was clearly an error.
10  His novels were once very popular but now they are all ................. print.

## Verb + preposition (1)

I   Complete the sentences with the correct preposition.

1   When you change jobs, you have to adapt .............. different systems.
2   We know each other well, so we can dispense .............. formalities.
3   They were charged .............. an offence under the criminal code.
4   What led you .............. that conclusion?
5   They withdrew .............. the agreement at the last minute.
6   If he insists .............. attending the meeting, we can't prevent it.
7   He always responds .............. criticism by losing his temper.
8   I find it easy to identify .............. her because I had a similar upbringing.
9   I don't approve .............. that sort of behaviour.
10  He's an obvious suspect, though he's never been convicted .............. a crime.

## Verb + preposition (2)

**J** Complete the sentences with the correct preposition.

1 The children vie .............. each other .............. their mother's attention.
2 The evidence conflicts .............. the official explanation.
3 Products must conform .............. European safety standards.
4 Their research contributed .............. the success of the project.
5 He gets very angry whenever anyone disagrees .............. him.
6 He is very reliable so I have no hesitation in entrusting the task .............. him,
7 I'm not sure if that law applies .............. foreigners.
8 I don't think this is the right moment to invest .............. shares.
9 I like going to the theatre, but that play didn't appeal .............. me.
10 Ever since he disappeared, the newspapers have indulged .............. speculation.

## Common combinations (adjective and noun)

**K** Complete the sentences, choosing the correct adjective or noun used adjectivally from the list below.

| common | continuous | fixed | foregone | mutual | narrow | pet | security | track | unknown |
|---|---|---|---|---|---|---|---|---|---|

1 There are no examinations. They use .............. assessment to decide which students pass.
2 They were over-confident before the game. They thought the result was a .............. conclusion.
3 The marriage was terminated by .............. consent.
4 Her appointment to the European Commission did not come as a surprise. Her relationship with the French Prime Minister was .............. knowledge.
5 He has quite a lot of money in the bank, apart from his .............. assets – the house and land, and so on.
6 I think Smith's the best candidate. He has an excellent .............. record.
7 On the other hand, Jones seems interesting, though he's something of an .............. quantity.
8 He was not given the job on the grounds that he was a .............. risk.
9 I don't like any of the members of this Government, but the Prime Minister is my .............. aversion.
10 I had a very .............. escape. I could have been killed.

## Common combinations (verb and noun)

**L** Complete the sentences, choosing the correct verb from the list given below in the most appropriate tense.

| change | cross | gain | make | pay | play | put | serve | set | take |
|---|---|---|---|---|---|---|---|---|---|

1 I never imagined I would win the prize. It never .............. my mind.
2 Like most politicians, if you ask him a difficult question, he just .............. the subject.
3 It's not a very attractive office, but it .............. its purpose.
4 You're the eldest, so we expect you to .............. an example to the others.
5 She was nervous at first, but once she got used to the system, she .............. confidence.
6 If you don't .............. attention to the teacher, you won't learn anything.
7 Everyone deserves congratulations. You have all .............. a part in our success.
8 You must .............. an effort to see his point of view.
9 The thieves .............. advantage of the owners being on holiday to get into the house.
10 They were making so much noise that I had to .............. a stop to it.

*Idiomatic phrases*

**M** Rewrite the sentences, using the correct phrase from those given. Where necessary, put the verbs into the correct form. Note that the sentences will have the same meaning as those printed but the order of words may change.

| a warning note | all the rage | be taken aback | club together | fall short |
|---|---|---|---|---|
| follow in (sb's) footsteps | follow suit | the done thing | the good old days | turn a hair |

**1**  I was astonished when she suddenly accused me of stealing.

I ................................................ when she suddenly accused me of stealing.

**2**  That would never have happened in the past, when things were better.

That would never have happened in ................................................ .

**3**  When the news came through, he resigned and his colleagues did the same thing.

When the news came through, he resigned and his colleagues ................................................ .

**4**  All the members of staff have made a contribution to buy her a leaving present.

All the members of staff have ................................................ to buy her a leaving present.

**5**  I'm afraid the performance did not come up to expectations.

I'm afraid the performance ................................................ of our expectations

**6**  Their records are very popular just now.

Their records are ................................................ just now.

**7**  It's not acceptable behaviour to attend a formal dinner without wearing a tie.

It's not ................................................ to attend a formal dinner without wearing a tie.

**8**  I've been successful as a writer, and now my son is pursuing the same career.

I've been successful as a writer, and now my son is ................................................ .

**9**  I thought it would upset her but she wasn't in the least worried.

I thought it would upset her but she didn't ................................................ .

**10**  The bad trade figures indicate possible risks for the economy.

The bad trade figures sound ................................................ for the economy.

**N** Rewrite the sentences, using the correct phrase from those given. Where necessary, put the verbs into the correct form. Note that the sentences will have the same meaning as those printed but the order of words may change.

| a weepie | as far as it goes | kick one's heels | light years | old times | plain sailing |
|---|---|---|---|---|---|
| poke ... nose | run the show | take a leaf out of ... book | the nanny state | | |

**1**  Once we got out of the city, the journey was free from trouble.

Once we got out of the city, it was all ................................................ .

**2**  What a pleasure to see you again! It's just like the way things used to be.

What a pleasure to see you again! It's just like ................................................ .

**3**  He was taken on as the boss's assistant but he ended up in charge of the business.

He was taken on as the boss's assistant but he ended up ................................................ .

**4**  The plan is satisfactory up to a point but it doesn't get to the roots of the problem.

The plan is all right ................................................ but it doesn't get to the roots of the problem.

**5**   I'm copying the Prime Minister, renting a villa in Tuscany.

I'm .................................. the Prime Minister's ........................... , renting a villa in Tuscany.

**6**   The children were bored, with nothing to do, until I found this old game upstairs.

The children were ............................................ until I found this old game upstairs.

**7**   Her latest film is a sentimental one aimed at making everyone cry.

Her latest film is .................................... .

**8**   The explanation they gave was very far from a true account.

The explanation they gave was ............................................ away from a true account.

**9**   They think citizens must be treated like little children.

They believe in ............................................ , where citizens are treated like little children.

**10**  As a result, they think the government has the right to interfere in everything we do.

As a result, they think the government has the right to ........................................... into everyone's business.

○   Rewrite the sentences, using the correct phrase from those given. Where necessary, put the verbs into the correct form. Note that the sentences will have the same meaning as those printed but the order of words may change.

| | | | | |
|---|---|---|---|---|
| *a far cry* | *be caught red-handed* | *be left standing* | *do a good trade* | *go through the roof* |
| *in pole position* | *make light of* | *old hat* | *out of one's hair* | *settle the score* |

**1**   When they choose a new leader, he'll be the first one to be considered.

When they choose a new leader, he'll be ............................................ .

**2**   We've been selling a lot of these souvenirs lately.

We've been ............................................ in these souvenirs lately.

**3**   It seemed a bad wound to me but he treated it as nothing serious.

It seemed a bad wound to me but he ............................................ it.

**4**   I had to think of something to stop the children getting on my nerves.

I had to think of something to get the children ............................................ .

**5**   The boss exploded with rage when I told him.

The boss ............................................ when I told him.

**6**   Life in the desert was a very different experience from life in the city.

Life in the desert was ............................................ from life in the city.

**7**   They were discovered at the scene of the crime, holding the jewels.

They were ............................................ , holding the jewels.

**8**   He was so far ahead of the rest of us that we couldn't compete with him.

He was so far ahead of the rest of us that we ............................................ .

**9**   His ideas are completely out of date nowadays.

His ideas are very ............................................ nowadays.

**10**  He's been looking for a chance to get his revenge ever since it happened.

He's been looking for a chance to ............................................ ever since it happened.

**P**    Rewrite the sentences, using the correct phrase from those given. Where necessary, put the verbs into the correct form. Note that the sentences will have the same meaning as those printed but the order of words may change.

> a double-edged sword     be left behind     carry ... weight     come to light     hold sway     make the best of
> make the most of     out of the public eye     the other side of the coin     window dressing

**1**    They've promised urgent remedial action, but that's just a comforting statement to keep people happy. Nothing will change.

They've promised urgent remedial action, but that's just ............................................. . Nothing will change.

**2**    He hasn't been seen in the newspapers or on television recently.

He's been ............................................. recently.

**3**    Your competitors will get ahead of you, if you're not careful.

You'll ............................................. , if you're not careful.

**4**    Those landowners have great influence in that part of the country.

Those landowners ............................................. in that part of the country.

**5**    He won the law case but the contrasting aspect of the matter is that he'll have to pay his own costs.

He won the law case but ............................................. is that he'll have to pay his own costs.

**6**    There's not much daylight left, so we'd better take full advantage of it.

There's not much daylight left, so we'd better ............................................. it.

**7**    He's employed as an expert adviser, but no one takes much notice of what he says.

He's employed as an expert adviser, but what he says doesn't ........................ much ........................ .

**8**    It was a disappointment, but the only thing to do was to take what we could out of the situation.

It was a disappointment, but the only thing to do was to ............................................. it.

**9**    Trying to please both sides in the conflict could prove to be a weapon that would turn against him.

Trying to please both sides in the conflict could prove to be ............................................. .

**10**   It was a long time before the fraud was discovered.

It was a long time before the fraud ............................................. .

**Q**    Rewrite the sentences, using the correct phrase from those given. Where necessary, put the verbs into the correct form. Note that the sentences will have the same meaning as those printed but the order of words may change.

> get in on the act     go all out     go through a bad patch     go with a bang     keep one's head down
> look on the bright side     make short work of     pick up the threads     sit on the fence     take sb for a ride

**1**    It's no good trying to compromise. You must try your hardest to win.

It's no good trying to compromise. You must ............................................. for victory.

**2**    They didn't waste any time dealing with the opposition.

They ............................................. the opposition.

**3**    It's time they intervened, instead of avoiding taking sides and doing nothing.

It's time they intervened, instead of ............................................. .

**4**    We want the celebrations to be lively and a big success.

We want the celebrations to ............................................. .

**5**     When people promise to make you a fortune, they're usually deceiving you.

When people promise to make you a fortune, they're usually ................................................ .

**6**     You're not very popular at the moment, so avoid attracting attention.

You're not very popular at the moment, so ................................................ .

**7**     They're sure to want to become involved in the business, now they can see the profit.

They're sure to want to ................................................ , now they can see the profit.

**8**     Let's be optimistic. It may not turn out to be as bad as we fear.

Let's ................................................ . It may not turn out to be as bad as we fear.

**9**     The team are not having the best of luck at the moment, but that will pass.

The team are ................................................ at the moment, but that will pass.

**10**    When I come back to work after the holiday, it takes me some time to get back to the normal routine.

When I come back to work after the holiday, it takes me some time to ................................................ .

**R**  Rewrite the sentences, using the correct phrase from those given. Where necessary, put the verbs into the correct form. Note that the sentences will have the same meaning as those printed but the order of words may change.

| | | | | |
|---|---|---|---|---|
| *by luck than judgement* | *change one's tune* | *do the trick* | *fall through the floor* | *get it into one's head* |
| *give rise to* | *sell sb a pup* | *the going is good* | *washout* | *wear and tear* |

**1**     His sudden disappearance caused people to speculate.

His sudden disappearance ................................................ speculation.

**2**     The best plan is to sell your shares while you're still making a profit.

The best plan is to get out of the market while ................................................ .

**3**     I'll try and open it with this knife. That should prove successful.

I'll try and open it with this knife. That should ................................................ .

**4**     Good fortune rather than skill was the reason why I won.

I won rather more ................................................ .

**5**     As soon as I buy a share, it goes right to the bottom.

As soon as I buy a share, it ................................................ .

**6**     I can't understand how you came round to believing that I was responsible.

I can't understand how you ................................................ that I was responsible.

**7**     Everyone spoke highly of him but in my view he's a total failure.

Everyone spoke highly of him but in my view he's a complete ................................................ .

**8**     I'm afraid they've tried to pass off something worthless on you.

I'm afraid they've tried to ................................................ .

**9**     He says he's delighted with it but I reckon he'll express a different opinion when he sees the bill.

He says he's delighted but I reckon he'll ................................................ when he sees the bill..

**10**    The policy doesn't cover damage caused by ordinary use.

The policy doesn't cover damage caused by normal ................................................ .

**S**  Rewrite the sentences, using the correct phrase from those given. Where necessary, put the verbs into the correct form. Note that the sentences will have the same meaning as those printed but the order of words may change.

| | | | | | |
|---|---|---|---|---|---|
| big break | flog a dead horse | flop | fly in the ointment | get rid of | go begging |
| hog the limelight | know no bounds | look down one's nose | over the limit | | |

1   When the news came through, there was no limit to his delight.

   When the news came through, his delight .............................................. .

2   His latest film was a total failure.

   His latest film was a .............................................. .

3   I'm going to dispose of this armchair. It doesn't match the rest of the furniture.

   I'm going to .............................................. this armchair. It doesn't match the rest of the furniture.

4   If the Prime Minister takes charge of the Queen's jubilee celebrations, he'll elbow her out of the way and try to be the centre of attention!

   If the Prime Minister takes charge of the Queen's jubilee celebrations, he'll elbow her out of the way and try to .............................................. .

5   The team were too slow to take advantage of their chances in the game.

   Chances in the game .............................................. because the team were too slow.

6   The magazine photographer was the one thing that spoilt the wedding.

   The magazine photographer was the only .............................................. at the wedding.

7   People are tired of hearing the same arguments so they're wasting their efforts.

   People are tired of hearing the same arguments so they're .............................................. .

8   Being offered that part in the film was her great opportunity.

   Being offered that part in the film was her .............................................. .

9   He has no cause to think himself superior. He's no better than the rest of us.

   He has no cause to .............................................. at us. He's no better than we are.

10   You can't drive a car in that state, sir. You've drunk more than is permitted.

   You can't drive a car in that state, sir. You're .............................................. .

T    Rewrite the sentences, using the correct phrase from those given. Where necessary, put the verbs into the correct form. Note that the sentences will have the same meaning as those printed but the order of words may change.

| | | | | |
|---|---|---|---|---|
| *call a spade a spade* | *call it a day* | *get tough with* | *make one's flesh creep* | *much fun* |
| *onto something* | *port of call* | *put a stop to* | *strike dumb* | *the lap of luxury* |

1    It's strange that people like hearing stories that make them feel nervous.

It's strange that people like hearing stories that ................................................. .

2    People imagine film stars live in great comfort, but they work very hard.

People imagine film stars live in ................................................. but they work very hard.

3    The news was so surprising that everyone was lost for words.

The news was so surprising that everyone was ................................................. .

4    That's enough work for now. It's time to stop.

That's enough work for now. It's time to ................................................. .

5    I need some aspirin so the first place I need to visit is the chemist's.

I need some aspirin so my first ................................................. will be the chemist's.

6    Being married to a man who's always travelling can't be very enjoyable.

Being married to a man who's always travelling can't be ................................................. .

7    I think you might have made an important discovery.

I think you might be ................................................. .

8    Politicians avoid saying what they really think. They never speak plainly.

Politicians avoid saying what they really think. They never ................................................. .

9    We're determined to take a firm line with people who break the law.

We're determined to ................................................. people who break the law.

10    People were leaving the office early but the new boss soon brought that to an end.

People were leaving the office early but the new boss soon ................................................. it.

# Appendix I     *Phrasal verbs*

Many of the items in tests of vocabulary are **phrasal verbs** (common verbs followed by prepositions, where the meaning is not immediately clear in the context). By this definition, *to be carried away* (moved by emotion) is a phrasal verb, but not when the words mean, literally, to be carried to a different place. There are a very large number of these verbs in English and many of them have more than one meaning, depending on the context.

This list, intended for reference, includes all those that occur in this book, but it is not complete and does not cover all the possible meanings of a verb. You should study it but also keep a notebook to write down any other phrasal verbs you may *come across* (meet by chance) in your reading.

Where a phrasal verb usually occurs in association with a particular subject – for example, health – I have indicated it in (brackets). Some of the verbs used are slang expressions. These are indicated as (infml).

| | |
|---|---|
| **back out of** | withdraw from |
| **bank on** | rely on |
| **blow away** | be carried away (by the wind) |
| **blow out** | extinguish, put out (flame) |
| **bowl over** | surprise and impress |
| **break down** | fail, collapse, stop working (marriage, car, health) |
| **break out** | escape (prisoners) |
| **break out** | start (war, disease) |
| **break through** | make new discoveries, overcome obstacles |
| **break up** | close down for the holidays (school) |
| **bring on** | cause to develop |
| **bring up** | look after and teach how to behave (children) |
| **bump off** | kill (infml) |
| **bunk off** | disappear suddenly in the direction of (USA, infml) |
| **call off** | cancel, abandon (event) |
| **call up** | order to represent (military service, national team) |
| **calm down** | become calmer or try to make others calmer |
| **be carried away** | become excited, be moved by emotion |
| **carry out** | do, put into effect |
| **cast aside** | abandon as useless or not wanted |
| **catch up with** | reach, overtake (car, past actions) |
| **catch up with** | arrest (crime) |
| **claw back** | recover, with great difficulty (money, social position) |
| **come about** | happen (usually unexpectedly) |
| **come up with** | think of, propose (ideas, plans) |
| **cope with** | manage, deal with, with difficulty |
| **crop up** | occur, by chance |
| **cut out** | omit, exclude |
| **die down** | become gradually less strong or noticeable (noise, rumours) |
| **die out** | disappear, become extinct |
| **do away with** | abolish, destroy |
| **do up** | decorate (house) |
| **dress up** | dress well (for a special occasion) |
| **end up** | reach, terminate (after a long period of time) |
| **face down** | confront and cause to give way |
| **fall off** | decrease, diminish (numbers, attendance) |
| **fall out** | quarrel |

| | |
|---|---|
| **fall through** | fail to be completed |
| **flag down** | wave at to stop (car, taxi) |
| **gang up on** | form a group to do harm to someone |
| **get away with** | escape punishment for |
| **get on with** | continue doing |
| **give up** | surrender (hope) |
| **go down** | be received (suggestions, performance) |
| **hack out** | cut out, with difficulty (path) |
| **hand over** | transfer to (goods, money, responsibility) |
| **hang around** | wait, stay without any purpose |
| **hang on to** | not let go of, refuse to give up |
| **hang over** | remain (as a threat) |
| **hem in** | surround, restrict movement of |
| **hit (it) off** | get on well with (relationship) |
| **hold out** | last (supplies) |
| **home in on** | move directly towards (target) |
| **jabber away** | talk excitedly |
| **jack in** | abandon (infml) (job) |
| **lash out** | try to hit, violently |
| **lay into** | attack violently (individual, group) |
| **live up to** | be as good as (expectations) |
| **live out** | spend the rest of one's life |
| **loaf about** | spend time idly, not doing anything |
| **look up** | improve (prospects) |
| **make out** | understand (meaning, handwriting) |
| **make up** | constitute |
| **make up for** | compensate for |
| **miss out on** | lose an opportunity to benefit from |
| **pay off** | prove justified, successful |
| **perk up** | become or make more lively (infml) |
| **pick up** | see, hear by electronic means |
| **play off against** | cause to compete with (each other) |
| **plonk down** | put down heavily (infml) |
| **point out** | indicate (fact, information, mistake) |
| **pour out** | express freely (feelings) |
| **price out** | make too expensive for |
| **prop up** | support by standing behind or under (physically and mentally) |
| **pull up** | stop, usually suddenly (car) |
| **put off** | cause to show less interest in |
| **be put out** | be upset, disconcerted |
| **put up** | raise |
| **put up with** | tolerate (something unpleasant or annoying) |
| **roll on** | may it come soon (infml) |
| **rub off on** | be transferred to (personal qualities) |
| **rule out** | exclude |
| **run along** | go away and play, amuse yourself (to children) |
| **run into** | meet by chance |
| **see off** | chase away |
| **send back** | return |
| **set apart** | make different from or superior to |

| | |
|---|---|
| **set off** | contrast and balance |
| **set off** | leave a place and start a journey |
| **set out** | leave on a journey, with an intention |
| **set up** | establish |
| **shake off** | escape from, get rid of |
| **sit through** | watch (something boring or unpleasant) patiently |
| **slip through** | get through without being noticed |
| **speak out** | express opinions clearly, without fear |
| **speed up** | increase or make something go faster |
| **spin out** | make something last longer |
| **splash out** | spend, without thinking or counting the cost |
| **split up** | separate (relationships) |
| **spring up** | appear suddenly |
| **stand for** | represent |
| **stand in for** | substitute for |
| **stand up to** | resist |
| **stem from** | come out of |
| **stir up** | provoke (trouble) |
| **stow away** | hide on board a ship to travel to another place |
| **strike down** | attack and incapacitate (illness) |
| **switch off** | use a switch to stop the flow of (see turn off) |
| **take in** | absorb, understand |
| **take off** | leave the ground (plane) |
| **take over** | take control of |
| **take up** | occupy (time) |
| **tip off** | warn secretly |
| **track down** | search for with determination and find |
| **trail round** | walk, following others |
| **turn into** | be transformed into |
| **turn off** | stop the flow of (water, gas) |
| **turn out** | prove (to be) in time |
| **turn up** | appear, when not expected |
| **watch out** | be careful, keep an eye on |
| **while away** | pass, entertaining oneself (time) |
| **whip through** | go through at great speed (reading) |
| **wipe out** | destroy |
| **work out** | do physical training exercises |

A number of vocabulary items in tests may be part of an **idiomatic phrase**. For examination purposes, it is necessary to learn and remember the phrase as a whole since only one part of the combination – the noun or verb or adjective – will be missing in context. But this is also the best way to learn them for general use because these combinations are the ones we use in everyday conversation, rather than words of similar meaning. For example, people who have been lucky not to be injured in an accident say they have had a *narrow escape*. They do not say 'a close escape' or 'a near escape'.

The list here is, of course, not complete but only refers to expressions used in this book, and to the meanings in context in this book, though others may sometimes exist.

Where an expression usually occurs in connection with a subject – health, for example – I have indicated it in (brackets). Some of these phrases are only used informally. These are marked (infml).

Note that the combinations are listed alphabetically as follows: adjective before noun (*narrow escape*, not *escape, narrow*); verb before noun or adverb (*know no bounds*, not *bounds, know no* and *lead astray*, not *astray, lead*).

| | |
|---|---|
| **all the rage** | very popular, in fashion |
| **at arm's length** | not close enough to be involved or friendly |
| **be caught red-handed** | be caught while committing a crime |
| **be left behind** | not make as much progress as others |
| **be left standing** | be outclassed by the opposition |
| **be onto something** | have information that may lead to advantage |
| **be struck dumb** | be so astonished that one is unable to react |
| **be taken aback** | be very surprised |
| **big break** | great opportunity (infml) (career) |
| **bloomer** | mistake (infml) |
| **blue-collar** | working-class |
| **booming** | doing very well (business) |
| **break-up** | collapse, separation (marriage) |
| **bunk** | nonsense (infml) |
| **call a spade a spade** | speak directly, saying what one means |
| **call it a day** | decide to finish, retire |
| **carry weight** | have an important influence |
| **a case in point** | a relevant experience or example |
| **change the subject** | talk about something else (because embarrassed, confused) |
| **change one's tune** | express oneself differently (usually in a less positive manner) |
| **clobber** | clothing or equipment, usually additional to needs (infml) |
| **club together** | join together for a purpose (collecting money) |
| **come to light** | be discovered, observed |
| **common knowledge** | something that is generally known (rumour, etc) |
| **diehard** | person strongly opposed to change |
| **do cow** | play the part of an unpleasant woman (v infml, actress's slang) |
| **do a good trade** | sell well, be popular with the public |
| **do the trick** | provide the solution |
| **the done thing** | the action accepted as correct in society |
| **a double-edged sword** | sth that has advantages and disadvantages |
| **drivel** | nonsense (usually spoken) (infml) |
| **drop-off** | indicates parents leaving children at school in the morning (infml) |
| **drop-out** | person who does not conform to society and leaves it |
| **economical with the truth** | official language for 'telling lies' |
| **fall short of** | not come up to expectations |

| | |
|---|---|
| **fall through the floor** | go suddenly to the bottom (business), collapse financially |
| **as far as it goes** | up to a point (but not entirely) |
| **a far cry from** | very different from |
| **few and far between** | rare and not often encountered |
| **flog a dead horse** | continue to do something when its value no longer exists |
| **flop** | failure (film, play, etc.) |
| **the fly in the ointment** | the one thing that spoils what is otherwise successful |
| **follow in the footsteps of** | copy, follow the same career (as parents, teacher, etc.) |
| **follow suit** | imitate, act in the same way |
| **a foregone conclusion** | a result that was evident before it occurred |
| **get in on the act** | take part, and not be excluded |
| **get it into one's head** | come to believe (curiously, without justification) |
| **get a bad name** | have a bad reputation |
| **get rid of** | dispose of |
| **get the bug** | develop enthusiasm for, interest in (infml) |
| **get tough with** | take a firm line towards |
| **give rise to** | cause to occur |
| **go all out** | make a total effort for |
| **go begging** | not be taken advantage of (opportunities) |
| **go through a bad patch** | experience a difficult situation, be in poor form |
| **go through the roof** | lose one's temper and be very angry |
| **go with a bang** | be a great success (celebration, party) |
| **the good old days** | time in the past (usually better than the present) |
| **guff** | nonsense (infml) |
| **out of their hair** | not getting in the way and being a nuisance (children) |
| **hard cash** | money (in contrast to promises, theories, credit) |
| **hit** | success (film, play, etc.) |
| **hit bottom** | go as low as can be expected |
| **hog the limelight** | want to be the centre of attention (infml) |
| **hold sway** | be dominant, control (an area, situation) |
| **keep one's head down** | stay out of trouble by avoiding attention |
| **kick one's heels** | move aimlessly, because bored, not knowing what to do |
| **know no bounds** | be very great, have no limit |
| **the lap of luxury** | very comfortable circumstances |
| **lead astray** | introduce someone to bad habits, actions |
| **lesser breeds** | inferior species (families, races) |
| **light years** | a very great distance |
| **look down one's nose at** | feel superior to, despise |
| **look on the bright side** | take an optimistic view |
| **low-lifes** | small-time criminals (infml) |
| **over the limit** | having drunk more than is permitted (drivers) |
| **on the look-out** | keeping one's eyes open for (opportunity) |
| **more by luck than judgement** | as a result of good fortune, rather than skill |
| **make the best of** | do as much as possible (in unpleasant circumstances) |
| **make one's flesh creep** | entertain by frightening |
| **make light of** | treat as not serious (accident, injury, problem) |
| **make the most of** | take full advantage of |
| **make short work of** | overcome, demolish very quickly |
| **moggy** | cat (infml) |
| **not much fun** | not very enjoyable (life, an experience, a companion) |

| | |
|---|---|
| **no mug** | not silly (infml) |
| **the nanny state** | government that does not trust individuals to look after themselves (infml) |
| **a narrow escape** | a fortunate escape from accident, injury, etc. |
| **an occupational hazard** | a risk common to a particular sort of work |
| **off-message** | out of touch with fashionable (political) ideas |
| **old-hat** | out of date and no longer in fashion (infml) |
| **old times** | the past (meetings, memories recalling the past) |
| **one-eyed** | biased, incapable of seeing the other point of view (infml) |
| **a pet aversion** | a person or thing particularly disliked |
| **pick-up** | collecting children from school at the end of the day (infml) |
| **pick up the threads** | return to the working routine |
| **plain sailing** | straightforward, causing no problems |
| **poke one's nose into** | investigate and interfere in others' business, lives, etc. |
| **in pole position** | the favourite, person most likely to succeed, be selected |
| **pooch** | dog (infml) |
| **port of call** | place to visit |
| **the prime suspect** | the person most likely to be responsible, guilty |
| **out of the public eye** | no longer featured in the news, magazines, etc |
| **put a stop to** | terminate bad behaviour, work practice, etc. |
| **run the show** | take charge of the situation |
| **a security risk** | someone who cannot be trusted by his country, company |
| **sell a pup** | pass off something inferior as genuine (infml) |
| **settle a score** | obtain one's revenge |
| **shoe-horning** | trying to fit things in any way that is possible (infml) |
| **the other side of the coin** | the contrasting aspect of the matter |
| **sink without trace** | disappear and be completely lost |
| **sit on the fence** | avoid taking sides in a dispute |
| **souped-up** | given extra power and speed (engines) (infml) |
| **stop dead** | stop suddenly and completely |
| **take a dim view of** | disapprove of |
| **take a leaf out of someone's book** | copy them |
| **take someone for a ride** | deceive them |
| **take steps** | take action |
| **track record** | past experience, action (business, sport) |
| **not turn a hair** | remain calm in a serious situation |
| **an unknown quantity** | person or thing that is unpredictable |
| **a warning note** | an indication of potential danger |
| **a washout** | a complete failure (infml) |
| **wear and tear** | damage caused by normal use (machines, clothes, etc.) |
| **a weepie** | a sentimental film (film slang, v infml) |
| **while the going is good** | now, before things become worse |
| **white-collar** | middle-class |
| **a will of one's own** | an independent attitude |
| **window dressing** | presenting facts in a misleading way that makes them appear better than they are |

# Appendix 3 *Collocations and common combinations*

In this appendix, I have listed the following that appear in this book: **collocations** (preposition + noun, such as *in advance*), **verbs** (active and passive) **customarily followed by a preposition** (*adapt to, be accused of*) and **common combinations**, whether of nouns (*a course of action*), verb + noun (*make an allegation*) or adjective + noun (*fixed assets*).

In some cases, other meanings may be possible. Explanations are given when the meaning is not obvious. In all cases, it is important to learn these combinations as combinations. In an examination, either part may be omitted and the right answer may depend on recognising the combination.

## COLLOCATIONS

**in agreement**
**under arrest**
**on arrival**
**in business**
**in circulation** (in use)
**on the contrary** (the opposite is true)
**in contrast (to)**
**in court**
**in danger**
**in decline**
**on duty**
**at the expense of** (with a corresponding loss of)
**at first sight** (when seen for the first time)
**on the grounds (of)** (as a reason or justification for)
**on hand** (nearby, and available)
**out of hand** (out of control)

**out of harm's way** (away from the risk of danger)
**in line (with)** (consistent with)
**along these lines** (in this way, form)
**in living memory** (in the memory of those still alive)
**in the long run** (after a time, eventually)
**out of print** (no longer available (of books))
**in pursuit (of)**
**in question** (being referred to)
**out of range** (too far away to be hit)
**out of reach** (where it cannot be obtained)
**in retrospect** (looking back, with hindsight)
**in one's right mind** (sane, not mad)
**at risk**
**to scale** (in the same proportion as in the original)
**out of the way** (away from the centre)
**under way** (in progress)

## VERB + PREPOSITION

**be accused of**
**adapt to**
**agree with**
**appeal to**
**apply to**
**approve of**
**be ashamed of**
**be blamed for**
**care for**
**be charged with**
**communicate with**
**compete with**
**conflict with**
**conform to**
**contribute to**
**convert into**
**disagree with**
**be discharged from**
**dispense with**
**be enthusiastic about**

**entrust to**
**be familiar with** (be used to)
**be guilty of**
**identify with**
**improve on**
**indulge in**
**ingratiate oneself with**
**insist on**
**invest in**
**be keen on**
**matter to** (be important to)
**object to**
**react to**
**refrain from**
**be relevant to**
**resign from**
**respond to**
**subject to**
**vie with** (compete with), **vie for (sth)**
**withdraw from**

## COMMON COMBINATIONS

**the argument holds** (it is valid)
**bear in mind** (remember)
**bear a relationship**
**bill of fare** (menu)
**break the rules**
**breed in captivity**
**the bulk of** (the greater part of)
**cloak failure** (disguise it)
**come first** (take precedence, be considered first)
**come in sight** (appear)
**come up to expectations**
**have confidence (in)**
**continuous assessment** (judging by regular work, not by examinations)
**course of action**
**crave the limelight** (want to be the centre of attention)
**cross one's mind** (occur to one, think of)
**current issue** (most recent issue of a publication)
**do the rest** (do what remains to be done)
**drive one mad**
**an element of truth**
**enter one's head** (occur to one, think of (see **cross one's mind**)
**fancy dress** (unusual clothes worn at parties, etc.)
**fast asleep**
**finds its way** (reaches (by indirect means))
**first impression**
**fixed assets** (things of value that are not countable, such as land, houses)
**gain confidence**
**as a general rule** (in the normal state of affairs)
**give way to** (yield to)
**hold tight** (hold firmly to avoid losing)
**humble circumstances** (a poor or modest situation)
**job description** (written description of what a job consists of)
**keep an eye on** (watch or check to make sure it is all right)
**keep hold of**
**keep in ignorance** (deliberately fail to inform)
**keep watch** (stay watching, guarding)
**be kindly disposed (towards)** (look at, consider favourably)
**the law of averages** (what generally happens)
**lay waste (to)** (destroy)
**lead to a conclusion**
**let alone** (apart from) (see **not to mention**)
**lose sight of**
**make an allegation** (accuse)
**make an effort**
**make an example of** (punish as a warning to others)

**make one's fortune** (enable one to become rich)
**make a point of** (emphasise)
**make sense** (seem logical)
**management course**
**marriage guidance**
**not to mention** (let alone, not counting (the most obvious example))
**mutual consent** (with the agreement of both sides)
**news coverage** (the extent of reporting in newspapers, on TV, etc)
**next to nothing** (hardly anything)
**normal circumstances**
**nothing of the kind** (nothing like it, of this type)
**pass a test**
**pay attention (to)**
**play a part** (contribute to)
**a positive attitude**
**put to death** (execute)
**put an idea (into one's head)** (suggest, propose)
**put one's trust in**
**raise a family** (bring up children)
**recover consciousness**
**run a risk**
**serve a purpose**
**set an example (to)** (show, to be copied)
**set eyes on** (see)
**set free**
**set a pattern** (establish a course to be copied)
**set to work** (start working (seriously))
**show interest (in)**
**a sigh of relief**
**stormy weather**
**be struck dumb** (be so surprised that one cannot speak)
**subject to revision** (which may be changed)
**take advantage (of)**
**take into consideration**
**take a firm line (with)** (be strict with)
**take first place** (take precedence, be considered most important)
**take in hand** (take responsibility for, look after)
**take note (of)**
**be taken unawares** (be taken by surprise)
**throw out a challenge** (issue it)
**at the top of one's voice** (as loudly as one can)
**transfer fee** (money paid when players change clubs, people change jobs)
**a vain hope** (one that has no chance of being fulfilled)
**(by a) wide margin** (by a considerable number of points, votes etc)
**the wisest course (of action)**
**the younger generation**